AF323738

The Collapse of the Soviet Empire

A View from Riga

George J. Neimanis

PRAEGER

Westport, Connecticut
London

Library of Congress Cataloging-in-Publication Data

Neimanis, George J.
    The collapse of the Soviet Empire : a view from Riga / George J.
Neimanis.
        p.   cm.
    Includes bibliographical references and index.
    ISBN 0–275–95713–6 (alk. paper)
    1. Soviet Union—Politics and government—1985–1991. 2. Russia
(Federation)—Politics and government—1991– 3. Soviet Union—
Economic conditions—1985–1991.   4. Latvia—Politics and
government—1991– I. Title.
DK288.N45   1997
947.085′4—dc20   96–24332

British Library Cataloguing in Publication Data is available.

Library of Congress Catalog Card Number: 96–24332
ISBN: 0–275–95713–6

First published in 1997

Praeger Publishers, 88 Post Road West, Westport, CT 06881
An imprint of Greenwood Publishing Group, Inc.

Printed in the United States of America

The paper used in this book complies with the
Permanent Paper Standard issued by the National
Information Standards Organization (Z39.48–1984).

10 9 8 7 6 5 4 3 2 1

For Naomi

Contents

1

Introduction: A View from the Periphery of the Soviet Empire

One of the tragedies of the Cold War—a principal reason it lasted so long—was that the Americans leading the fight vastly overrated the enemy because they had never seen his homeland.

—Richard Reeves,
"Eastern Europe a Circle of Hell,"
The Buffalo News, August 9, 1993

I

June 1991. The few passengers for the Soviet Aeroflot flight from Helsinki to Riga had to board a bus to reach the Ilyushin airliner parked some distance away from the terminal building. In comparison to the glistening giants bearing Lufthansa, Scandinavian Airlines, and Finnair logos, the much smaller Soviet plane appeared humble inside and out. The floor coverings, seats, and luggage racks had a well-worn look that one associates with genteel poverty, where items are repaired but seldom replaced. After many years of use, floors, walls, and furniture—what the ads for household cleaners call "environmental surfaces"—no longer appear clean no matter how often they are scrubbed.

As the plane taxied to the runway and then stopped before taking off, the backrests of the unoccupied seats collapsed forward, making a considerable noise that startled the passengers. As the plane gathered speed to get off the ground, the backrests snapped back to the upright position. Pretty soon the stewardess started to serve cupfuls of what she called "juice," a somewhat exalted name for a beverage obtained from boiling apples and spices in water. It was a popular drink in the USSR.

Our flight lasted about forty-five minutes. The Riga airport had very few planes in sight, and most of them were military. Numerous military installations clustered around the airport, but a group of soldiers seen in the distance did not seem to be doing anything at all. Soon we encountered another group and then another. In Soviet airports, one could never get far away from the Red Army.

After disembarking from our Ilyushin, we had to walk between two sparse rows of soldiers, each armed with a submachine gun, for about 300 yards to the terminal building. The military guardians of the airport chatted among themselves and appeared totally disinterested in us. Inside the customs shed, taciturn officials worked very fast while another group of armed soldiers lounged around. Nobody's baggage was opened, nobody was detained or questioned. Porters, who suddenly appeared in the ostensibly restricted area, pleaded for tips in convertible currencies. Offers of rubles elicited very ungracious responses.

During my first hours in Riga I kept wondering who had told us in the United States that they, the Soviets, were our match. In the run-down airport one did not see a single computer terminal or a special purpose vehicle that abound in Western airports. The route to my hotel wended through a dilapidated city inhabited by shabbily dressed people who drove old cars. During the twenty minutes drive I counted four cars that had broken down along the road and whose drivers endeavored to fix them on the spot. After a few days of drabness, the eye longed to see something new: a new building, or streetcar, or bus, or automobile, but none appeared. Once I unintentionally insulted my hosts by observing that the general appearance of things made it difficult to believe that anything of good quality could be produced here. It was a tactless and not altogether accurate remark; nonetheless, products or services of high quality were rare in the USSR. As it turned out, accumulated low quality can destroy an empire.

II

The twentieth century almost turned out to be the Soviet century. Since its birth-revolution in 1917, the Soviet Union profoundly influenced, sometimes decisively shaped, world politics, wars, economic development, and intellectual currents. After the victory in World War II, the USSR reached its zenith of power and entered the second half of the twentieth century as a master of a constellation of satellites. It fell apart in 1991.

Throughout its seventy-four years, the Soviet Union suffered as well as created much violence, but the collapse came almost peaceably and hardly qualified as a revolution. But while the startling process was going on, nobody called it inevitable or predicted its outcome.

In a sense the easy collapse of the USSR diminished its adversaries, who for decades had expended enormous amounts of resources and mental energy in maintaining readiness for a showdown with the ostensibly mighty evil empire. As a percentage of what was available, the Soviets expended even more resources keeping ready to repel the impending capitalist onslaught. Clearly all governments had made enormous miscalculations, but so had the academics, who trained future politicians and intelligence analysts; journalists, who reported and interpreted current events; and writers, who supplied background information.

Until 1991, no publication in the West suggested that the strength of the USSR was an illusion and that its planned economy had foundered. Strident arguments that the Soviet system had failed came from Soviet emigrés, but it was widely agreed that their almost pathological anticommunism beclouded their judgment. For the emigrés with various accents, the failure of Soviet communism was an old saw, but they, too, did not foresee its sudden collapse.

A failure on the scale of that of the USSR must have had multiple causes. The Soviet success in concealing their problems and catastrophes from the outside world and from their own people was one of them. Under the Soviet regime, the leadership at all levels seldom learned from experience because failures and shortcomings were consistently denied. The public media reported and the education system substantiated and legitimized the reports that the USSR, under the enlightened leadership of the Communist party, marched from success to success. According to the Soviet press and official statistics, no serious accidents, no serious crime, and very few natural disasters marred the triumphant march forward. If mistakes are the best teachers, then the Communist Party of the Soviet Union (CPSU) had none because officially the party of Lenin and Stalin (after 1956 Lenin only) made no mistakes. That is why Khrushchev's speech at the Twentieth Party Congress in 1956, in which he revealed and denounced Stalin's crimes, absolutely stunned the party members. Serious and conforming men and women had been offered a glimpse of the devil who, in the guise of the "cult of personality," lurked behind communist altars and shrines. The notion that the Party could make serious errors went against the grain of nearly everybody, and during Brezhnev's reign (1964–1982) the Party again assumed the mantle of infallibility. Nevertheless, the purges, repressions, and the millions of lives extinguished during Stalin's era had left a legacy of fear of strong personalities, the fear of another Stalin.

Ironically, the Soviet system did poorly as an example of Marxism put into practice. Marx postulated that the prevailing "mode of production," the comprehensive set of ways and means by which a society produces goods and services, ultimately determines all social, political, and even spiritual relationships. The mode of production adopted by the Soviet state—central planning, collective farming, state ownership, and centralized management of the production and distribution systems— resulted in ubiquitous genteel poverty for the masses and relative affluence ("privilege") for the numerous officers, officials, and bureaucrats, the Soviet *nomenklatura*, necessary for running everything from above. (The *nomenklatura* was the list of all positions of significance controlled by the Communist party.)

Initially the planned command economy gained some notable victories. Heavy industry of vast size came into being. Wide canals intersected difficult terrains, and the virgin lands in the arid steppes were at least intermittently cultivated. New industries created new cities, and the size of the Soviet military-industrial complex ranked either as first or second in the world. In space, the Sputnik preceded the earliest American manned spacecraft.

But the profound industrial and technological progress never created a sufficiency of consumer goods and services. The standard of living got stuck in communal apartments and long lines at stores. The postwar recovery did not provide a modicum of luxuries to the population, and by the 1970s, stagnation had replaced rapid growth. The economy badly needed repairs.

The never-ending privation and want gradually corroded faith in socialism. Stalin's successors were not men of iron. They lacked the ruthlessness necessary for sealing off Soviet borders and air space, and images of Western affluence slowly seeped in. At some point it became apparent that the Soviet propaganda about penury in the West was a pack of lies that formed but a part of an all-embracing system of official lying. Deadly cynicism replaced idealism and the willingness to bear sacrifices for the roseate future of communism. The *nomenklatura* showed the way by greedily accumulating goods that remained unavailable to the ordinary builders of socialism.

Ultimately, economic failures as well as maldistribution of incomes and privileges are caused by human beings who, according to Marx, are molded by the prevailing mode of production: Its modern name is *the system*. The Soviet system turned out to be incapable of selecting people for key positions who were good at what they did. The party bureaucracy developed its own momentum and hierarchy of values in which loyalty to the party stood at the top. It recruited people who were ambitious, obedient, and ideologically correct; talent was secondary. Every loyal bureaucrat, being accountable only for attitude and never for results, could look forward to a lifetime of appointments. Georgi Arbatov, a shrewd observer of Soviet politics from the inside, remembers nobody being called to account for wrong decisions, in part because each decision required approvals numbering in dozens and sometimes in hundreds. The party shielded its incompetents by controlling criticism and by transferring them, as necessary, to new places or positions where they were temporarily unknown.[1] Nobody had to work very hard, but alienation— another Marxian term—from work and personal responsibility created cancerous inefficiencies that ultimately killed the system.

In the non-Russian republics, nationalism waxed as the economy floundered and Soviet power became hesitant. By the end of the 1980s, the new openness (*glasnost*) revealed to the Soviet people and the world that the moderate economic reforms (*perestroika*) had failed. More radical reforms called for the abolishing of the central plan. The diminution of central control implied increased local control, and in the non-Russian republics, demands for cultural and political autonomy accompanied economic reforms. In the Baltic area, Lithuania declared independence in 1990, while the Estonian and Latvian Soviet Republics started to act as independent states, clearly on their way out of the Union.

The mighty USSR had lost the good will and the confidence of its people. In August of 1991, six old men in high positions organized a putsch to restore the floundering system. The masses and the army did not respond. The people judged the system not worth maintaining.

III

The USSR was by far the largest country in the world, extending over eleven time zones for some 4500 miles east and west and by some 2300 miles north and south. Generally, Westerners observed it from the two open cities, Moscow and Leningrad (now St. Petersburg)—that is, open to foreigners. The Soviet government used to exclude foreigners from many parts of the country, and where travel was permitted, prolonged residence was not. The typical Western diplomat, journalist, or scholar lived either in Moscow or Leningrad and was allowed occasional sojourns to other cities and regions. Starting in about 1987, travel and residence restrictions were relaxed until they largely disappeared, enabling Westerners to study the Soviet Empire not only from its center but also from its periphery.

My vantage point was Riga, the capital of the Latvian Soviet Republic, now an independent state. In 1990, I had responded to a newspaper ad for Latvian-speaking economists, and between June and December of 1991, during a sabbatical leave from Niagara University, I found myself working as an economic advisor to the Economics Committee of the Latvian parliament. Later on, I spent the summers of 1993, 1994, and 1996 in Latvia, this time primarily as a visiting professor of economics at the Riga Business School. This is not a book of reminiscences. Personal experiences merely tie together and help to illuminate fragments in a chain of events: the breaking up of the USSR, which seemed so startling then and appears inexorable now.

NOTE

1. Georgi Arbatov, *The System: An Insider's Life in Soviet Politics*. New York: Times Books, 1992, pp. 223–224.

2

Poverty of Flesh and Spirit

There has been and remains a shortage of everything: metal, fuel, cement, machinery, and consumer goods. Our economic mechanism, whether we like it or not, is geared to mediocre or even substandard work.

> —Mikhail Gorbachev, speech to the Nineteenth All-Union Conference of the Communist Party, June 28, 1988

The political economy of socialism is stuck with outdated concepts and is no longer in tune with the dialectics of life.

> —Mikhail Gorbachev, *Perestroika: New Thinking for Our Country and the World.* New York, Harper & Row, 1987

I

To paraphrase Leo Tolstoy, "All poor families are alike but a rich family is rich after its own fashion." As the twentieth century entered its last decade, most families in the USSR were poor by comparison with the United States, Canada, the Scandinavian countries or any member of the European community. They were not poor by the standards of Bangladesh, Zaire, or Afghanistan. The communist ideal of equality had been largely realized, but it looked as if people had purchased their belongings in second-hand stores. Their poverty was not dramatic. Emaciated, hollow-cheeked children with huge eyes did not beg for food in the streets, and nobody died of starvation. Instead, the shortage-shaped economy made it difficult to replace things, and the various possessions of Soviet citizens and the Soviet state had become shabby, threadbare, faded, dilapidated, decrepit, and seedy. Ubiquitous genteel poverty does not provoke outrage. A TV reporter whose camera lingers on damaged walls, empty light bulb sockets, rusty cars, and chipped dishes bores rather than outrages.

Statistical studies confirm a relatively low standard of living in the USSR during its last decade. Western estimates show the 1985 USSR per capita consumption as 29 percent of the U.S. level. On a comparative scale , that placed the USSR below Portugal (32 percent of the U.S. level) and above Turkey (20 percent of the U.S. level).[1] The last Soviet statistics were less sanguine, estimating the 1985 per capita consumption between 22 and 26 percent of the U.S. level.[2] The average consumption levels did not disclose the severely limited consumer choices. At any one time, if available at all, there were only one or two washing machine models in stores, one kind of TV, four kinds of radios, etc. Theoretically, a car buyer could choose among a Zhiguli, a Volga, a Moskovich, or a Lada. Realistically, the limited supply reduced the choice to one model only, most frequently the humble but reliable Lada. Purchasing of the more luxurious models required good connections. Money alone was never enough.

On technical grounds, statistical comparisons of the USSR with the United States are difficult due to differences in methodology and what Professor Ericson from Columbia University calls "systemic incentives for exaggeration and ideologically and politically motivated distortions"[3] in the USSR. Perhaps under *perestroika* and *glasnost* purposeful distortions diminished, but past sins carried over to future time periods. Actual or suspected lying by Soviet statistics agencies had damaged public confidence in the published data. Every official number allegedly included a"socialistic premium."

Economists and government officials in the Latvian Republic tacitly dismissed the data produced by their own State Statistics Committee. In a sense, the official numbers did not matter because nobody used them for any important purpose. Interestingly, officials of the ministerial rank and above claimed to have their own private statistical data, which they apparently did not share with one another. Nobody, not even the central planners, had access to the supersecret monetary statistics. The record of rubles in circulation was kept in a single, hand-written copy inside a safe at the Republic's branch office of the USSR Central Bank.

The effectiveness of economic planning depends in a large measure on reliable statistical information. But that was one of the shortages in the USSR. The political process had become curiously "number-less" as ministers and members of the parliament felt quite comfort-able working with a minimal amount of statistical information. Early in the summer of 1991, I participated in a session of the Economics Committee of the Latvian Supreme Council (parliament), at which a government department requested an increase in the budgetary appropriation. No analysis of expenditures, revenues, the rate of inflation, or projected trends encumbered the department's request. Their argument rested on this: "We need a little more money: inflation, you know." When numbers lose meaning and reliability, words are preferred.

II

From a birds-eye view of the USSR, every retail and service establishment dangled from a line made up of extraordinarily patient human beings. Early in the morning, as the working population wended its way to offices and factories, lines had already formed in front of nearly every retail establishment. Especially long were the early morning lines at food stores — the fear being that by 10 o'clock everything would be sold out.

Lines came in all kinds of lengths; in some of them a person stood longer than a day. It worked something like this: A citizen needing to notarize a document arrives at the state notary office in the morning and takes a place in line. There are laws of the line. After standing for at least half an hour, it is socially acceptable to tell the person ahead of you and the person behind you to hold your place in the line because you have very urgent business elsewhere. Then every two hours or so you must return to renew your position in the line. In the evening, when the office closes, people go home only to restore the line the next morning in the same order as the night before. Large families were fortunate because they often had a retired member who could stand in lines full time. There are few large families in Latvia, and newspapers periodically printed stories of young couples who had hired a grandfather or grandmother of a different family to stand in lines for them.

Veterans of the Great Patriotic War (i.e., World War II) used to have the right to go to the front of every line. This meant, in effect, that military retirees—there are tens of thousands of them—did not have to stand in lines even though many of them had not served in World War II. Since the 1980s, that custom has been terminated by one of the first successful grassroots action in the USSR. With harsh words and threats of physical violence, civilians in the lines began chasing the alleged veterans to the end of the lines. Perhaps on orders from above, the police (militia) did not interfere, and egalitarianism triumphed over military privilege.

When the shopper ultimately reached the head of the line, she (sometimes he) faced rude service and very limited choices. Frequently what she needed had been sold out and the time spent in line had been wasted. Every store had an abundance of sales clerks, but the lines would have been much shorter had the sales clerks been efficient, took shorter breaks, and talked less among themselves. Undoubtedly shoppers had ceased to notice, but the Soviet retail organizations had the peculiar gift of making the ambience unattractive and the merchandise unappealing. That did not matter because by and large Soviet shoppers bought whatever was available. Some items were not available at all (a glaring example was the assortment that in American drugstores is shelved in the section for feminine hygiene). The country with the largest expanse of forests in the world had difficulties in producing a sufficient quantity of paper goods. Only the better restaurants supplied paper napkins, measuring 4 by 4.5 inches, to their customers. I never saw any paper towels at all.

Whereas retailers in the West strive to attract customers, every Soviet state store in 1991 tried to serve only the residents of its district. The tool for weeding out unauthorized buyers was the "visiting card," issued by the municipal authorities. Only card carriers were authorized to buy in a particular store. The authorities hoped, always in vain, that the administratively delimited demand would match the scanty supply available. Actually stores did not enforce the visiting card requirement very diligently. Most sales clerks did not really care who bought.

The state stores fulfilled one-half of the Soviet ideal: Prices were kept low. However, the other half, a plentitude of all goods, never materialized. Soviet citizens could also shop at the farmers' markets and commission stores, where supply and demand set the prices. Farmers' markets offered a wider selection of fruit, vegetables, meats, fish, and dairy products than did the state stores, but the prices were appreciably higher. For example, in early July of 1991 in Riga, fresh strawberries in the state stores sold for about 1.50 rubles for half a kilogram, while prices in the farmers' markets reached about eight rubles. But the harvest turned out to be excellent, and for once strawberries in the state stores were plentiful. Quite soon the free-market price also dropped to 1.50 rubles for half a kilogram.

Free-market retailers sometimes combined to fix prices. The most colorful monopolists in Riga were sellers of dried fruit and nuts from the Soviet Asian republics. These street merchants, distinguishable by their colorful beaded caps, formed a closed unit policed by grim-looking young men with leather jackets who made sure that no price competition would take place.

Farmers' markets were perfectly legal. By contrast, some of the very numerous commission stores operated beyond the margin of legality because their merchandise had been expropriated from the state store supplies. An item priced at five rubles at a state store disappeared and somehow found its way to a commission store, where the price was fifteen rubles or more. The population generally believed that in retailing, private enterprise could be trusted to be unethical.

Stories of coping with diverse shortages made up a large part of the saga of everyday life in the USSR. To an outsider, the never-ending list of deficit items, a Soviet euphemism for shortages, soon became repetitious and dull. Was there nothing available in adequate quantities? Most of the time bread was plentiful and inexpensive. Indeed, the price was so low that people, against the advice of veterinarians, used bread to feed cows, goats, and sheep. Public transportation, too, was inexpensive and reliable. Government offices had an unlimited supply of excellent, white, unruled bond paper and paper clips. Unavailable at all or in very short supply were pens, pencils, erasers, pencil sharpeners, ruled writing pads, scotch tape, rubber bands, spare parts and supplies for copiers, index cards, desk calculators, desk lights, light bulbs, and telephones. Retail establishments and banks had plenty of abacuses but few cash registers or adding machines.

In the economies of modern, advanced countries, any shortages are supposed to be temporary. Shortages in the Baltic Republics began with the Soviet occupation in 1940. In Russia, shortages began during World War I and never completely disappeared throughout the subsequent triumphs of communism. Many middle-aged men and women had never tasted a banana and never lived with indoor plumbing. In 1991, *Wartime Kitchen* was the most popular cookbook sold in Riga's bookstores, but there had been no war for forty-seven years.

Amid ubiquitous shortages, quality was not "job number one." Soviet manufacturers concentrated on fulfilling the plan, and no plan set a high priority on quality or on catering to the tastes and conveniences of individuals.

A common spectacle on streets and highways was the mechanical breakdown of cars. Neither auto makers nor dealers extended any guarantees or warrantees. The buyer of a new car arrived at the state showroom accompanied by a mechanic, who would make sure that the brand-new vehicle could be driven home. The dealer only collected money: The full price of the car. No product liability laws existed in the USSR. Finding the right spare part for anything required time, endurance, good connections, and luck. The owner of a mechanical or electrical device purchased any spare part available, for parts could always be traded.

Under favorable circumstances, construction of new buildings took five to fifteen years. But after a decade under construction, even nominally new buildings looked weathered and lived-in. Despite critical shortages of living space, numerous structures remained unfinished while the huge cranes alongside slowly rusted out. Plans had gone awry.

Nothing arrests the aging process of buildings, but maintenance does help to slow it down. As there was no private ownership of apartment buildings, who maintained them? In theory the state, in reality nobody. In theory, building superintendents served as the link between tenants and the municipal authorities, who controlled the maintenance organizations, or "brigades," of plumbers, electricians, painters, and carpenters. Except for cases of the direst emergency, (e.g., a ruptured water main), requests for repairs remained on the waiting list for months and even years. When the repair technicians finally arrived, their skill level often turned out to be low. Tips always improved workmanship, but the workers' state did not require or make sure that workers be skillful.

Buildings, too, require spare parts: window glass, light bulbs, replacement doors and windows, etc. None of this was readily available. As a result, most windows in hallways were broken, light bulbs were missing, and many of the ornate front doors that were scorched during the World War II Battle of Riga in 1944 had not been replaced. In late June, I noticed for the first time a missing manhole cover on one of the main downtown streets in Riga. The big, round hole in the pavement posed an obvious and serious safety hazard. Some days a wooden pole protruded two or three feet above the opening as a warning to the traffic, but it never stayed in place for long as somebody always removed it. On November 18, five months later, a steel cover finally eliminated the safety hazard. To the best of my knowledge, the open manhole caused no accidents.

The law did protect the rights of renters. One's apartment or room in a communal apartment was not exactly private property, but the law made eviction very difficult. This created one of the incongruities of life in the USSR. The hallway of a tenement building is dirty and smells of urine. The stairs are rickety, many window panes are cracked or missing, and no artificial light helps the visitor to locate the right apartment number. The a door opens to a bright and attractive apartment, lovingly kept up by its renter. One learns that artists, engineers, university professors, and physicians live in this partially dilapidated building. The dilapidated part— the hallway and the stairs —"belong to the people," while the illusion of private ownership sustains the well-maintained part, the individual apartments.

The small apartments are jammed chock full of furniture, books, TVs, record players, and household appliances. By and large, two bedrooms and a kitchen per family was the norm. The upper layer of the *nomenklatura* lived in special buildings under the protection and surveillance of police detachments. Reputedly, these apartments were modern and spacious, but I never gained admission to one of them.

In 1991, about one-third of the Soviet urban population lived in communal apartments. Nothing has provided more material for the Soviet satirical literature than life in communal apartments, where two to four families share a single kitchen, a single bathtub, and a single toilet. The perpetual sharing of living space opened one's social skills and earthly possessions to a minute and not always friendly scrutiny by fellow apartment dwellers. Human relations within a communal apartment worsen when hot water is available only at night and sometimes on Sundays. Every five-year plan promised an individual apartment for every Soviet family, but millions of communal apartments still exist in what is now the former USSR. In the 1980s, the waiting period for a private flat used to be eight to twelve years, which discommended prospective marriages and depressed the birth rate. Many men stayed away from their depressing communal apartments as often as possible; mothers with young children could not exercise that option.

Communal apartment came into being as a result of rapid urbanization. Under the Soviet rule, the primarily agricultural Russia became the primarily industrial USSR. The populations of all major cities doubled and tripled in size. Moscow, a city with 4.1 million residents in 1939, had become a city with 8.8 million residents by 1986. The population of Kiev, the capital of the Ukraine, grew from 846,000 in 1939 to 2.5 million in 1986, and the population of Tashkent, the capital of Uzbekistan, grew from a little over half a million in 1939 to 2.1 million in 1986. The population of Riga increased from 348,000 in 1939 to 915,000 in 1989. The Soviet construction industry could not keep up with the demand for apartments, and it did not take into consideration the demographic structure of the population. Living space in the cities became the primary shortage in the USSR. The location and the size of the apartment largely determined the quality of life of a Soviet citizen and his or her status in society. People who had apartments held onto them at all costs. In Latvia in 1989, 176,000 people continued living in officially condemned buildings.[4]

The government responded to the persistent shortage by administratively allocating living space. In Riga, the allotment in the 1980s was 8.7 square meters per person. That worked out to one room, approximately 14 by 14 feet per individual. A larger room would have to be shared by two or more individuals.

The construction industry built numerous two- and multistory apartment buildings of identical designs. The materials used were manufactured hastily, with no variety and little regard for quality. The buildings did not weather well, especially in cold climates. The planners set the norms for the construction industry in square meters. Whether a floor of an apartment building had four or eight apartments did not change the total number of square meters. Bathrooms and toilets, the "sanitary-technical block," made the construction process more cumbersome. Time and materials could be saved, and bonuses earned, by economizing on the sanitary-technical blocks; the fewer the better. Construction brigades preferred to build three-, four-, and five-room apartments. Unfortunately, out of every 1000 families in Latvia, 378 had only two members[5] and therefore qualified only for a two-room apartment. Two such families could be squeezed into one four-room communal apartment.

Riga, Moscow, and Kiev are old cities. Apartments in the buildings constructed before the Soviet era typically had four to eight large rooms with high ceilings. Very few families—75 out of 1000 in Riga[6]—

qualified for five rooms. Communal apartments again provided the solution. In the spacious old buildings, three or four families per apartment were not uncommon.

III

The party line extolled women. The Soviet woman could do anything, accomplish any task: design engines, run factories, perform brain surgery, investigate crime, cut lumber, pave streets, and drive trucks and tractors. There was no bias, no discrimination on the basis of sex. But the Soviet ideology was superimposed on a society that made a very clear distinction between the traditional men's and women's jobs. In the olden days, men worked in the fields from sunrise to sunset while women prepared food, made cloth, and took care of animals and children. Eventually industrial occupations replaced plowing, sowing, and reaping for most males, but nothing replaced the female jobs at home, except that for working women the time available for household chores was compressed into those hours that extend late into night. Only for males did the industrial age provide more leisure. Irrespective of the prestige of her occupation, the Soviet woman stood in lines for food, cooked, cleaned, sewed, and took care of children without much male assistance and without many labor-saving appliances. Very slow washing machines were fairly common, but only homes of the elite had clothes dryers, dishwashers, and microwave ovens. Household tasks became even more burdensome when, due to a breakdown or malfunction of the municipal heating plant, water needed to be heated on the stove for bathing children and washing dishes, and when a family had the use of only one burner on the stove and one cabinet in the kitchen of a communal apartment.

For the Soviet woman who could do anything, including taking care of her family, the workday routinely began at 6 a.m. and ended at midnight. The pressures of never-ending chores frequently led to neglect of health. As one physician observed, a woman makes an appointment at the clinic, a diagnosis is made, and a treatment is prescribed, but she does not show up for the follow-up visit. Her excuse: I don't have time.[7] For many women, the appearance of old age without teeth began in their forties. For ordinary people, the access to professional dental care meant many hours of waiting in lines. The USSR had a very large number of physicians, about 50 for every 10,000 people versus 21 in the United States. Dentists, on the other hand, were a deficit item, with one dentist per 10,000 people[8] compared to 5.5 per 10,000 in the United States.

At work, women did enjoy certain privileges. Everybody realized that a woman's job is to get food for her family; therefore, she must stand in many lines. Shipments of food and other goods did not reach stores on a regular schedule. A woman employee might understandably arrive late because coming to work she (and other women) had discovered something worth buying; or standing in lines might extend her lunch period; or she may have to leave early to catch some fast-disappearing item somewhere in the distribution channels. In a society where people habitually hoarded information, women—comrades in the common cause of gathering food—formed an efficient network willingly passing on to one another any news about what was being sold where.

No feminist movement took root in the USSR, except for the conviction that males are more fragile than females. Women knew that men had difficulties in coping with life, as confirmed by their horrible alcoholism and ten years shorter average life span.

Males probably received more knocks from the system than did females. Soviet organizations practiced extremely primitive human resources management. Virtually everybody in charge seemed to enjoy the cruder exercises of power. More often than not, bosses screamed at their subordinates, threatened, and humiliated them. Typically the objects of the particularly brutal forms of leadership were men. Women, by virtue of being women and occasionally even addressed as "ladies," encountered rudeness more often than degradation. After a couple of decades of life in the USSR, mere rudeness rolled off one's sensibilities like water off the proverbial duck's back. The fragile and dispirited males craved mothering, which many women began during the courtship period and did not stop for the rest of their lives (i.e., they spoiled their men).

Women showed pluck in the face of daily shortages and rudenesses. They persisted in trying to create a somewhat aesthetic life. The female population of the USSR, particularly in the Baltic Republics, used up enormous quantities of fresh flowers, supplied to cities mostly by private vendors even during the most repressive periods. Flowers bought en route to work enlivened drab offices; flowers bought on the way home brightened crowded apartments. Women also strove, desperately, to dress well.

The secret of dressing well consisted of skillful alterations. The stylish Riga lady was either an excellent seamstress herself or knew someone who was. New garments could be fashioned out of old skirts, blouses, and coats by turning them inside out. A new sweater could be reknitted using the unraveled wool of old sweaters. Ingenuity and patience went a long way toward overcoming shortages. Respect for and interest in folk art, inculcated at home and in school since early childhood, helped to develop craftsmanship and good taste. Old fashion magazines from Paris and Germany kept on circulating throughout the female network. There was, of course, a perennial shortage of sewing supplies such as thread, sewing machines, needles, zippers, and buttons.

Because most wives and mothers were not skilled in tailoring men's clothing, a male whose wardrobe included more than one suit was probably a foreigner. In 1991, it was easy to spot a Latvian male. For the past five or six years, the state stores in Latvia had carried about a dozen different neckties, and the only shoes available were either battleship gray or light yellow. They stood out next to the black and brown shoes of foreigners. Moreover, shoe polish had not been available for decades, not even to the Red Army officers.

The system survived on people's ignorance of alternatives. The quality of Soviet cars and home appliances was low. To a Western palate, the common sweets, cakes, and cookies tasted insipid and a little salty due to the shortages of sugar and spice, yet the local consumers found them marvelous. Having had no international comparison, Latvians and Russians regarded many inferior products as excellent, modern, or tasty. Had they known the truth—had they had a comparison—the empire would have collapsed sooner.

IV

It is quite possible to fool most of the people most of the time, provided that the state devotes enough resources to the task. For the Soviet leaders, insulating the people from the outside world was a necessity for staying in power because a persistent genteel poverty becomes a tolerable standard of living only if the population can be made to believe that every other country is worse off.

It is difficult to keep a large population closeted, but the Soviet government tried very hard. Mail was censored and letters from abroad containing "anti-Soviet material" never reached the addressee. Radio broadcasts from the West were jammed, not always but intermittently. Western books and periodicals were available only in the reading rooms of special libraries for the purposes of authorized research and propaganda. Translators of foreign books and plays edited the original texts, making sure that they conformed to the proper ideological standards. Passages in books depicting, for example, prosperity of working men in the West had to be excised. The relatively few foreigners who received visas to enter the USSR were kept under constant surveillance by concealed microphones and cameras indoors, and by secret police agents outdoors. Placing almost the entire country off limits to foreigners facilitated controls. A Westerner had very few unsupervised moments. The state security organs registered all typewriters and controlled all duplicating machines. In offices, written communications had to be written by hand and then forwarded to the closely supervised typing and duplicating pool for transcription. After working hours, all typewriters and duplicating machines were locked up. A market for portable typewriters and personal computers did not exist in the USSR.

Those Soviet citizens who were allowed to visit Western countries were either quite old or regarded as politically reliable. The KGB additionally insured a person's return home by keeping his or her family in the USSR. Families tend to defect together, whereas individual members usually returned home. But even politically reliable travelers to the West had to undergo character guidance sessions in preparation for dealing with Western propaganda and, so it was asserted, the omnipresent Western intelligence services. Soviet women were particularly warned about Western agents in the U.S. beauty salons.

After Stalin's death, controls gradually diminished and with *glasnost* and *perestroika* almost disappeared. As some old men and women complained, Comrade Stalin's successors were weaklings and traitors who traded away patriotism and order for unpatriotic, selfish, and destructive liberties. Indeed, Comrade Stalin did know how to keep the window to the West shut. After World War II, most Soviet prisoners of war were shipped directly to labor camps to quaranteen the rest of the population from any Western influences the men might have picked up in the German prisoners of war (POW) camps.

The old travel restrictions have left an aftertaste of suspicion. Today, all those who had traveled to the West before 1990 are suspected as having been KGB spies. The policy of closed borders had other lasting consequences. One of them still is the dearth of foreign language skills. Soviet authorities used to declare with pride that foreign languages, especially English, were widely taught in high schools. Unfortunately, the motivation to learn was absent. Why struggle with English language instructions if there was no hope of traveling to the West or reading English books and periodicals? The only language worth learning was Russian.

Geography lessons in schools kept reminding the young and their parents of places in the world they would not be allowed to visit. Children memorized the names of foreign capitals and the sizes of foreign countries—every one of them, it was pointed out, smaller than the mighty USSR. Clearly the West existed and had to be portrayed somehow. The Soviet intellectual authorities proceeded by exaggerating the weaknesses of Western political and economic systems—above all, the inequality of income distribution. The young learned in school that under capitalism, a small wealthy class cruelly exploits the working class. Unemployment is very severe, with a quarter to a third of the labor force continually out of work. The masses cannot afford the necessities of life. Streets overflow with beggars and criminals, both groups being the victims of capitalism. The working-class slums are riddled with disease because only the wealthy can afford medical care. There used to be a story that all school children had heard because all of them were exposed to the same textbook, the only one authorized by Moscow. An old American couple is sitting at a table on the morning of their twenty-fifth wedding anniversary. "I have a wonderful present for you," says the husband to his wife. "Your wedding ring is finally paid for."

The negative portrayal of the West asserted that the capitalist ruling class prevents revolution by employing a vast network of police and intelligence services spies. People are not told about the progress of socialist society in the USSR. But there is hope! The communist parties in the West are getting ever stronger and better able to defend the interests of the working class. Furthermore, while the police and state security agencies keep workers' aspirations and love for the USSR in check, the military and industrial complex is waiting for the opportunity to attack the motherland of socialism. Soviet citizens can expect an air-raid alarm at any moment (this was most often told to school children). Only the vigilance of the Red Army, Navy, Air Force, and the incorruptible KGB keeps the capitalist war dogs at bay.

Did people believe the tales of exploitation, want, and ferocity in the West? They believed them more in some places, less in others, and perhaps least of all in the Baltic Republics, where virtually everybody had relatives in the West. Nevertheless, it is impossible to dismiss everything one has been taught since the first day in school.

In 1991 it seemed strange that the core of the diatribes against capitalism came almost verbatim from the writings of Karl Marx, especially *Das Kapital I*, published in 1867. One would think that modern critics of capitalism should be able to come up with something more recent. On the other hand, the tortuous course of Soviet intellectual history amply demonstrated the danger of quoting politically incorrect authors. Many a man and woman of letters paid a high price for quoting Trotsky and Bukharin after Stalin came to power, quoting Stalin after Khrushchev came to power, quoting Khrushchev after Brezhnev came to power, and quoting Brezhnev—the stagnationist—after Gorbachev came to power. Only Marx, Engels, and Lenin remained safe, and of the three Marx is the most extensive and most vitriolic critic of capitalism.

In the Baltic States, the Soviet occupation in 1940 stopped the progress of economics and other social sciences. Almost immediately, sciences scurried back to the life and times of Karl Marx, who (as every Soviet citizen knew and everybody else should know) by the time of his death in 1883 had discovered all the inexorable laws of history and society. The demolition of the bourgeois social science became the principal task of university professors and members of the Academy of Science. Reading a 1980s textbook on industrial economics, one discovered that every chapter contained attacks on capitalism. It would have been a better textbook if the author had demolished capitalism in the first chapter and then focused exclusively on industrial economics in the subsequent chapters, but that was not the way Soviet textbooks were written.

In the summer of 1991, a Riga newspaper printed an article in which the author, a doctor of economics, wondered whether Marx's accounts of the satanic mills of capitalism were not somewhat erroneous. By contrasting the writings of Karl Marx (1818–1883) with those of Henry Ford (1863–1947), the author admitted the possibility, in 1991, that capitalism may have evolved differently from what Marx had predicted. The author was not a communist and therefore had never been allowed to step outside the Soviet realm. The point, however, is that doctors of economics in the USSR knew next to nothing about Western economies and economic science. Economics inside the Soviet Union had become a mixture of nineteenth century Marxism and cybernetics with a smattering of linear programming thrown in. The mixture of the very old and new was odd and not at all useful for running a business or an economy.

How did people piece together a personal, distinct from the official, picture of the West? In Latvia, shortly before and during World War II over 200,000 Latvian citizens escaped to the West, ultimately settling in the United States, Canada, Australia, West Germany, Sweden, Great Britain, and other countries. The State Statistics Committee estimated the 1989 population of ethnic Latvians in Latvia as 1.4 million. Two hundred thousand is about 14 percent of 1.4 million. Virtually every Latvian family had relatives in the West. About a million people of Lithuanian descent live in the United States, and a large number of Estonians escaped to Sweden during the last months of World War II. Emigration stretched but did not sever family ties. During the darkest days of Stalinist repression, many families learned somehow whether or not their relatives abroad were alive. A few letters and packages from the West started to arrive in the early 1950s, and gradually careful communications via the mail became commonplace. More than just a few isolated personal visits to Latvia began in the 1970s, and by the late 1980s hotels in Riga started to fill up with foreign tourists, not all of them of Latvian descent.

In the late 1980s, restrictions of travel outside the USSR were relaxed until money rather than politics became the main obstacle to visiting Western countries. But the vigilant KGB never slept, and as late as in 1990 and the early part of 1991, certain Soviet citizens could not obtain visas to get out, and certain foreigners could not obtain visas to get in. For a long time the KGB tried to ensure that no unauthorized printed matter would enter and no manuscript would leave the USSR.

Official travel abroad was always authorized to selected Soviet officials, scientists, artists, and athletes. Among perquisites of office and achievement, travel to the West ranked above a *dacha* and the thirteenth-month salary. The KGB accepted as a fact of life that the luggage of official travelers coming home from the West would weigh more than the luggage with which they had departed. Veterans of military service in Eastern Europe, Africa, and Afghanistan formed another group that had seen the world outside the USSR.

Travel within the Soviet bloc had far fewer restrictions than travel to the West. Even for ordinary Soviet citizens, excursions to East Germany, Poland, Hungary, Czechoslovakia, Bulgaria, Romania, and sometimes North Vietnam were feasible and not particularly expensive. By comparison, the satellite countries were more Westernized and more affluent than the USSR, and Soviet citizens came back lugging heavy suitcases filled with goods unavailable at home.

By the late 1980s, the hard-currency stores, found in the larger cities, occupied a special place in the Soviet retail chain. They offered a wide variety of imported goods as well as local handicrafts that might tempt foreign tourists for payment in U.S. dollars and other major Western currencies. In Riga, most of the sales staff spoke English or German and treated their customers with courtesy uncommon in state stores. It was amazing to see how many Soviet citizens possessed foreign currencies.

Western radio broadcasts used to tantalize Soviet citizens. For many years listening to anything but the official voice from Moscow remained a forbidden fruit. Despite occasionally heavy jamming, the BBC, Voice of America, Vatican Radio, Radio Free Europe, Radio Liberty, Deutsche Welle, and others managed to get through. In one area the West scored an impressive early victory: Among the youth, rock music became as popular in the USSR as in Western Europe.

Among the Baltic Republics, Estonia presented an impossible challenge to the Soviet authorities. The Finnish and Estonian languages are very similar, and only the forty-mile-wide Gulf of Finland separates the Estonian capital Tallin from Helsinki. Despite the great expenditure of resources, it was impossible to isolate Estonians from the Finnish radio and TV. Farther to the south, Lithuania benefitted from its contiguity to Poland, except that the Polish language is quite different from Lithuanian and that Poland was a Soviet satellite while Finland was not.

Gradually the Baltic peoples developed a fairly clear picture, not about life in the West, but about the differences between their own poverty and Western affluence. The Russians in Russia, unlike the nationalities along the western periphery of the empire, were less conscious of Western lifestyles and affluence due to fewer relative abroad and more effective jamming of radio waves. Nonetheless, the empire was supposed to be homogeneous and information within it diffused freely. Whatever was known in Tallin, Riga, or the Lithuanian capital Vilnius soon became known in Moscow and beyond. As for Moscow, it always had more foreigners than any other place in the USSR, and what people learned in Moscow soon spread to those other places. However, there are remote villages in northern Russia where nothing much has changed since the freeing of serfs in the 1860s and where information from any place arrives sporadically and late.

V

The Chernobyl nuclear accident mirrored the main symptoms of the pervasive sickness that ultimately brought down the USSR: (1) the perfection and infallibility of the Soviet system by definition; (2) extreme secrecy irrespective of its consequences; (3) widely diffused managerial responsibility; (4) shortages; and (5) people placed in responsible positions who were not very good at their work.

A little past midnight on April 26, 1986, at the V. I. Lenin Nuclear Power Station in Chernobyl, during an overdue and mismanaged test, operators turned off safety systems. The ensuing uncontrollable power surge caused an explosion of the number 4 reactor. The roof or "biological shield" blew off, and fire in the reactor core burned for several days. The explosion released some fifty tons of radioactive substances into the atmosphere. By comparison, the atomic bomb dropped on Hiroshima weighed under 4.5 tons.[9] Fire and radiation killed thirty-one people, while 204 were hospitalized with very serious burns and radiation poisoning and about 500 more for significant radiation exposure.[10] Estimates vary, but somewhere between 92,000 and 135,000 residents had to be evacuated from the thirty-kilometer exclusion zone around the nuclear power plant.[11] Several million people in the Ukraine and the Byelorussian Republic were exposed to unsafe levels of radiation, and instruments recorded heightened levels of radioactivity in the atmosphere as far away as the United States and Japan.

According to the Soviet ideology, taught at schools, sermonized about at the workplace, and monitored by the party apparatus, scientific socialism, by virtue of being scientific, was immune to systemic failure. The communist party, represented by the politburo and the general secretary, never made mistakes, while the ever-vigilant KGB rooted out foreign intelligence agents, corrupt individuals, and saboteurs before they could do any serious damage. Nearly everybody agreed that the somewhat disturbing "cult of personality" had ended with Stalin's death in 1953. Consequently, the Soviet press, published statistics, textbooks, monographs, and scientific papers never reported or analyzed failures or setbacks. As a result, nobody learned from mistakes because the authorities did not permit the acknowledgment of adverse experiences. It appeared that no serious accident ever disturbed life in the USSR.

Perhaps nothing in the USSR was accepted with greater confidence than the dictum that the generation of nuclear energy was absolutely safe. Distinguished academicians lent scientific authority to the assertion that nuclear power stations were safer "than the simplest of samovars."[12]

In the West, too, distinguished men and women celebrated the clean and supposedly safe atomic energy as the best hope for humankind. But at the same time, equally distinguished men and women cautioned against nuclear accidents and pointed to the unsolved problem of radioactive waste disposal. The Soviet Union spoke with one voice because the authorities brooked no dissent. On May 9, 1985, the Minister of Energy, Anatoly Ivanovich Mayorets, issued an order: "Information about [the] unfavorable ecological impact of the energy-related facilities (the effect of electromagnetic fields, irradiation, contamination of air, water, and soil) on operational personnel, the population, and the environment shall not be reported openly in the press or broadcast on radio or television."[13] In the academic press, Anatol Alexandrov, the president of the Academy of Science and director of the Kurchatov Institute, and Valeri Legasov, first deputy director of the Kurchatov Institute, made sure that the journal *Atomenergo* printed no articles that dealt with safety.[14] In a climate of absolute safety, such articles would be a waste of valuable journal space.

The Kurchatov Institute, named after Igor Kurchatov, the father of the Soviet atom bomb, developed all Soviet nuclear programs, from nuclear weapons to nuclear reactors for generating energy. The Institute operated under the Ministry of Medium Machine Building, a euphemism for a department of the KGB charged with the manufacturing of nuclear weapons.

The military connotations of atomic energy reinforced the secrecy surrounding and permeating nuclear power stations. Special interior ministry troops guarded them from the outside, while inside each reactor unit operated in nearly complete isolation from other units. This senseless secrecy created dangers:

Accidents were hidden not only from the general public and government but also from the people who worked at Soviet nuclear power stations. Mishaps were never publicized; and as nobody knew about them, nobody could learn from them. For thirty-five years people did not notify each other about accidents at nuclear power stations, and nobody applied the experience of such accidents to their own work. It was as if no accidents had taken place at all; everything was safe and reliable.[15]

Alexander Akimov, a shift foreman of the lethal Fourth Reactor Unit, had calculated the probability of a serious accident a 1 in 10 million per year. Akimov died on May 10 from burns and radiation suffered during the accident.[16]

The knowledge-numbing secrecy vitiated safety awareness and safety policies. At the time of the accident, the staff at Chernobyl had very few dosimeters on hand for monitoring levels of ambient radiation. Moreover, after the explosion, the radiation levels inside the building went above 800 roentgens per hour, but the available dosimeters could not measure radioactivity above 4 roentgens per hour. More powerful dosimeters had been issued, but they were locked up in a safe that got buried under the rubble.[17]

Operators lacked respirators and protective tablets of potassium iodide. The medical center lacked radiometric apparatus capable of identifying the nature and extent of external irradiation.[18] In short, the long-standing official assumption of the perfection and infallibility of the Soviet nuclear power generating establishment prepared no one for a serious accident.

Numerous organizations exercised jurisdiction over nuclear power stations. As all other Soviet enterprises, nuclear power stations worked under one-year and five-year plans. The All-Union Industrial Department for Nuclear Energy approved these plans while being monitored from above by the All-Union Ministry of Energy and Electrification. The Scientific Research Institute of Technical Energy Construction, under the umbrella of the Kurchatov Institute, designed nuclear reactors. Above them loomed the secretive KGB Ministry of Medium Machine Building. Then there was the State Committee for the Use of Atomic Energy and the All-Union Research Institute for Nuclear Plant Operations.

Party organizations paralleled all government organizations. At the top stood the nuclear power department of the Central Committee of the communist party, at the bottom the party committee of each nuclear power station. In addition, the general staff of the Red Army and the commander of chemical troops maintained surveillance over installations dealing with atomic energy.

Chernobyl is located in a corner where the USSR republics of Byelorussia and the Ukraine met. Kiev, the capital of the Ukraine and the third largest city in the USSR, lies less than sixty miles to the south. The powerful Ukrainian communist party and the Republic's government kept a close watch on Chernobyl. The much smaller interest shown by the Byelorussian communist party and government was due to the geographical fact that Minsk, the capital of Byelorussia, lies more than 200 miles from Chernobyl. Actually, 70 percent of the escaped radiation ultimately fell on Byelorussia.[19] After the explosion, Stanislas Shushkievicz, professor of nuclear physics at the Byelorussian Institute for Nuclear Energetics, reported higher levels of radiation in the Gomel region, some eighty miles from Chernobyl, than was officially acknowledged. The authorities responded by confiscating his instruments. In 1991, he became the first president of the independent republic of Belarus.

Immediately after the explosion, nobody on the spot felt able to authorize the evacuation of the nearby residents or the shutting off the adjoining reactor units 1, 2, and 3. These decisions had to come from Moscow. The evacuation was authorized the next day, approximately 33.5 hours after the accident, by Boris Scherbina, the Deputy Chairman of the Council of Ministers of the USSR.

The explosion occurred during a test that was seriously bungled by the operating personnel. But the test had been a part of the plan, and the failure to fulfill the plan carried penalties. Victor Brukhanov, the director of the Chernobyl Nuclear Power Station, had submitted the program of the test to his superiors in January of 1986. According to Medvedev, neither approval nor disapproval was ever received.

The government commission charged with investigating the accident overlooked flaws in the reactor design, the lack of coordination among the various agencies, or the poor enforcement of safety procedures. The brunt of the fault was ascribed to human failure at the operator level. Six individuals, including Brukhanov, received prison terms from two to ten years. All were released early. The system remained unchanged, but some officials were reprimanded and demoted. The chief of the All-Union Industrial Department for Nuclear Energy was fired and expelled from the Party.

The investigating committee made a great deal of the laxity and indolence of the operating personnel, who had been seen reading novels and playing cards. In reality, many of them had nothing to do. Chernobyl was hugely overstaffed having seventy persons per shift versus ten to fifteen in the United States. Only a few of them belonged to the elite Group of Effective Control that actually ran the station.[20]

The Soviet policy of zero unemployment in a workers' state succeeded in overstaffing all enterprises and offices. The nuclear power stations faced additional, more or less private pressures to enlarge their staffs. Employees lived in the nearby special cities, where life was good compared to the rest of the country, with well-stocked stores, cinemas that showed the latest movies, modern sports and cultural centers, and, most important, short waiting lists for apartments. These young cities had no communal apartments. Moreover, the industry paid well, its prestige stood very high, and, as everybody had learned, the work posed no safety hazards. The personnel departments of nuclear power stations were not inflexible in the face of pressures to create jobs for friends or relatives of well-connected persons. As a byproduct, many underqualified people held management and safety positions. Continuous education was not enforced.

The Soviet planned economy always had problems with synchronization. Deliveries arrived late, inputs received did not meet technical specifications, and quality standards varied among enterprises. Soviet managers, tied to a rigid plan, became masters of improvisation by necessity. But ingenious improvisation, admirable in the production of most goods, could be downright dangerous in the nuclear power industry, where the technical parameters must remain inviolate. The shipments of inputs necessary for the production of atomic power carried the highest priority, while the supplying of safety equipment did not. Some common items were not available at all. Employees never received individual dosimeters for monitoring the levels of ambient radiation.

As numerous crumbling buildings throughout the USSR testify, the Soviet construction industry, or construction materials industry, or both were incapable of maintaining high standards. Completion of construction projects ahead of the plan resulted in bonuses and medals but also in shoddy workmanship, even in building nuclear power plants. The system tolerated and rewarded people who were not very good at what they did.

For the cleaning up of Chernobyl, the Soviet government employed active army troops and mobilized some 200,000 reservists. Most of them were given cotton uniforms and gauze respirators.[21]These men, too, did not receive individual dosimeters.

For the Soviet public, the details of the nuclear accident emerged slowly and laboriously. Initially, the authorities' instinctive reaction was silence, except for a brief announcement in the government's newspaper *Izvestia* on April 29. Gorbachev publicly discussed the accident for the first time on May 14, two and a half weeks after it had happened. He stressed the heroism of firemen, technicians, scientists, and the military personnel. But the Chernobyl accident was one of those events that, like Khrushchev's speech at the Twentieth

Party Congress in 1956, disclosed to the Soviet public a failure of the Soviet system. The media had practiced cover-up and lying while high officials disregarded the health and safety of the people. The trials that followed placed nearly all the blame on the operating personnel. The system remained infallible by definition, but the definition was becoming less and less credible.

NOTES

1. Abram Bergson, "The USSR Before the Fall: How Poor and Why." *The Journal of Economic Perspectives*, Fall 1991, p. 31.

2. Ibid., p. 33.

3. Richard E. Ericson, "The Classical Soviet-Type Economy: Nature of the System and Implications for Reform." *The Journal of Economic Perspectives*, Fall 1991, p. 11.

4. *Statistikas gadagrāmata '89* (Statistical Yearbook for 1989). Latvian State Statistics Committee, 1990, p. 104.

5. Ibid., p. 26.

6. Ibid.

7. Dr. Edīte Lazovska, lecture, Toronto, October 3, 1993.

8. *Statistikas gadagrāmata '89*, pp. 131–132.

9. Grigori Medvedev, *The Truth About Chernobyl*. New York: Basic Books, 1991, p. 79. Grigori Medvedev was a Soviet nuclear engineer who had spent most of his career operating and supervising nuclear reactors. In the early 1970s he had been the Deputy Chief Engineer at Chernobyl. Twelve days after the accident he was appointed to a government fact-finding mission and spent eight days at Chernobyl.

10. Robert P. Gale and Thomas Hauser, *Final Warning: The Legacy of Chernobyl*. New York: Warner Books, 1988, pp. 174–175.

11. Ibid., p. 133.

12. Medvedev, p. 207.

13. Ibid., p. 20.

14. Piers P. Read, *Ablaze: The Story of the Heroes and Victims of Chernobyl.* New York: Random House, 1993, p. 21.

15. Medvedev, pp. 20 and 39.

16. Read, p. 43.

17. Medvedev, p. 136.

18. Ibid., p. 168.

19. Read, p. 288.

20. Ibid., p. 45.

21. Josh Karlen, "Baltic Survivors of Chernobyl Accuse Governments of Neglect," *The Baltic Observer*, March 23–29, 1995.

3

Nationalism and the Subversive Cemeteries

The building of Communism means creating a new phase in the relationships among the various nationalities in the Soviet Union. It manifests itself in an increasing closeness en route to a complete equality. The construction of the material and technical basis for Communism will weld the Soviet peoples ever closer together.

Nonetheless, the elimination of national differences, especially the elimination of different languages, is a process that will take longer than the elimination of class differences. Russian, however, has already become the common language in the relationships and cooperation among the Soviet peoples.

—Program of the Twenty-second Congress
of the Communist Party of the Soviet
Union, October 1961

I

Marxism has never come to terms with nationalism. Marx's and Engels's prophetic-sounding pronouncements that "the working men have no country" or "nationality is already dead" turned out to be hollow phrases by 1914 when German, French, and British working men enthusiastically enlisted under the flags of the Kaiser, the Republic, and the King. The Soviet regime tried to create a *homo sovieticus*, equally at home anywhere in the vast empire. But the language of the new Soviet man was to be Russian, and perhaps only people from the three Slavic republics—Russians, Russianized

Ukrainians, and Byelorussians—felt like genuine *homo sovieticus*. The more than 100 other nationalities in the empire looked at them as alien oppressors at the worst and privileged vagabonds at the best. After the death of Lenin in 1924, the Communist Party of the Soviet Union became a purely Russian institution, and in terms of Russian nationalism, the Moscow of the commissars was no different from the Moscow of the tsars: one faith, one language, one tsar—the faith being communism, the language Russian, and the tsar the General Secretary of the Communist party. In discussions about the non-Russian nationalities, the question always was what to do with them, *not* what they themselves wanted.[1]

Among the Soviet peoples, in theory all equal to one another, Russians were supposed to be "the older brothers." The Party made sure that the older brothers flooded the non-Russian lands by granting them two privileges: a good job and, most important, an apartment. The local populations bitterly resented this. Many of the new settlers, fully accepting the identity of *homo sovieticus*, never understood why. They asked, "Aren't we all Soviet people?" The unequivocal answer, usually whispered by the other nationalities, was "No, you are Russians and we are not." The *homo sovieticus* turned out to be a term of opprobrium designating primarily the quality of individual rootlessness.

The polyglot nationalities inside the old USSR perceived history as a struggle between the oppressors and the oppressed, where Russians had usually oppressed non-Russians. A strong case can be made that the Russian people, too, had been most cruelly oppressed by their own governments. Nonetheless, the source of the oppression makes a crucial difference. Under a foreign oppression, people clamor first and foremost for freedom, whereas citizens under the yoke of their own government crave justice and civil rights. The cry for freedom does not have resonance in countries like the United States or Great Britain, which have not seen foreign occupation for centuries. The public concerns in these countries address issues of civil rights, equal opportunities, and the equality of justice for all. People who live under a foreign occupation want political and cultural independence first and would be quite tolerant, at least initially, toward their own native oppressors. No matter how despotic the tsars of the commissars, they never forbade the Russian language or discommended the Russian culture. Indeed, the development of a specifically Soviet culture took the form of Russian cultural imperialism, which diminished the subjugated languages and cultures. Therefore, the struggle against Soviet oppression, occupation, domination, or colonialism—the terms used differ among the non-Russian nationalities—also meant the struggle for the survival of native languages and cultures.

Marxism and nationalism share one common element: the unimportance of the individual. Nationalism focuses its vision on the nation, Marxism on the class. Every individual is first and foremost a member of a nation or a class, and his or her whole being is subordinated to and owes allegiance to the nation or the class. For a nationalist, individual freedom grows out of national freedom, and individual dignity accompanies national dignity. Oppressive governments are the ones imposed by foreign invaders and occupiers. Individual freedom has no separate and transcendental meaning. Nationality is destiny.

II

The question of whether the Baltic States were occupied or liberated by the Red Army has been settled in favor of occupation despite Soviet denials. Apart from the various guerilla movements, World War II was fought by a rather small group of large nations: Germany and Japan on one side, the USSR, China, and the Western Allies on the other. The theaters of operations ranged over many smaller countries that were intermittently occupied and liberated. Whether to regard a country as occupied or liberated called for a political judgment. Did the Soviet Union occupy or liberate Czechoslovakia? Did Japan liberate or occupy Burma? In vernacular, the good guys liberate, the bad guys occupy. The Baltic States fell prey to the armed forces of the USSR and Nazi Germany. Neither one behaved like the good guys, and neither one ever liberated another country in the sense of letting it go its own way after liberation.

The Baltic Republics' history as part of the Soviet Union was comparatively short. Occupied by the Red Army and forcibly incorporated into the USSR in 1940 and occupied, in turn, by the Wehrmacht in 1941 and reoccupied by the Red Army in 1944 and 1945, Estonia, Latvia, and Lithuania were derided by upright communists as radish republics: red skin, white core. Only stern policies would keep the Baltic States (or Balts) in their place inside the USSR because for most of them, aspirations toward independence rather than ideas of democracy or capitalism formed the white core of anticommunism.

Throughout most of their history, all Soviet nationalities have lived in the shadow of Russia, and until the twentieth century many Westerners regarded them as part of the amorphous mass of Russian peasantry. Consequently, their nationalism—asserting a separate identity based on a distinct language and culture—had to be somewhat anti-Russian.

Russia acquired the Baltic provinces from Sweden and Poland between 1710 and 1795. Indigenous national movements building a national consciousness appeared in the middle of nineteenth century. At that time the Baltic peoples had a short history but a long prehistory. Hardly anything had been written about them, but over a million folksongs, tens of thousands of fairy tales, folk music, and magic formed a rich oral tradition that had to be organized, written down, and systematized. This body of folklore laid the foundations for Baltic literature and art as well as for their articulated nationalism.

Three sovereign Baltic States emerged at the end of World War I that had laid low, temporarily, two of their former masters: Germany and Russia. Baltic diplomats had considerable difficulties in convincing the Americans, British, French, and Italians at the Versailles Peace Conference that there existed, in fact, three distinct Baltic nations that culturally and linguistically differed from Russia.

Estonia, Latvia, and Lithuania declared independence in 1918 and fought a war with Soviet Union and Germany to keep it. Their statehood lasted until 1940. Other Soviet nationalities fared less well. Armenia, Azerbaijan, Georgia, and the Ukraine also declared independence after World War I, but their sovereignty did not last beyond 1921, when they were incorporated into the USSR.

The Baltic States started out as parliamentary democracies, but by the 1930s all three had come under the authoritarian regimes of Konstantin Päts in Estonia, Kārlis Ulmanis in Latvia, and Antanas Smetonas in Lithuania. By the standards of the twentieth century, the Baltic dictatorships were very mild, but they did profess a passionate nationalism. It did not take a belligerent form. Songs and poems called men to defend their fatherland instead of invading somebody else's fatherland. The nation, however, should occupy the central position in everybody's life, a desideratum that made the generally well-treated minorities (Russians, Jews, and others) a little alien among patriotic Estonians, Latvians, and Lithuanians.

Nationalism cannot be inculcated into the young without heroes as role models. In the process of becoming one, a national hero must overcome, or at least stand up against, formidable antagonists. For many of the Baltic heroes the antagonists had been Russians. Many of those who had fought the Red Army in 1919 and 1920 were still alive in 1940 when the Russians came back.

Western democracies frequently see nationalism as the breeding ground for intolerance toward other ethnic groups and religions, but national trauma (i.e., great suffering shared by multitudes) makes nationalism a self-defense mechanism as people of a nation pull closer together against an alien foe. Under the Soviet occupation, the Balts lived through two periods of massive deportations. In June of 1941, tens of thousands were arrested and shipped to Siberia. Eight years later in March of 1949, the number of deportees reached 100,000. These deportations were ordered by the authorities in Moscow and were carried out by the secret police, NKVD, a predecessor of the KGB, with assistance of the local party officials. The deportations aggrandized the fear of the authorities represented by the secret police but it also widened the chasm between the Russian-speaking establishment of the USSR and the non-Russian populations. Individual arrests and deportations continued throughout the period of the Soviet rule. The last Estonian president, Konstantin Päts, arrested in 1941, died in an NKVD psychiatric hospital in 1956. The Latvian president Kārlis Ulmanis died in a Russian prison in 1943.

There were two periods of guerilla war against the Soviet power. The first one came after the deportations in June of 1941, when the Red Army was retreating from the German forces. The second period lasted from 1945 until 1953. Of the three Baltic countries, Lithuania had the best organized partisan movement, which inflicted considerable casualties on the Soviet military forces, local party officials, as well as Lithuanian collaborators. It may seem totally unrealistic now, but the nationalist partisans or "forest brothers" were sustained by the belief in an impending war between the USSR and the Western Allies. In the course of such a conflict, the Baltic States would surely regain their independence. A hopeless but courageous struggle by abandoned people against overwhelming odds is the stuff nationalistic legends are made of. According to one Lithuanian,

Lithuanians remember it [the guerilla war] in every agonizing detail, and can no more stop talking about it than can the Russians stop talking about their great struggle against the Nazis.[2]

The Baltic nationalism was and still is highly romantic. Anatol Lieven, in his book *The Baltic Revolution*, calls it an "unreflecting" idealization of the past. It proved to be highly elastic, remaining subliminal during periods of intense repression but expanding rapidly as the rules from Moscow relaxed. Unavoidably, Baltic nationalism collided with the Great Russian nationalism in its form of unrelenting Russification. For nationalists, Russification was a greater evil than communism.

III

In the language of the Communist party, educating the working class in the spirit of internationalism meant Russification, "a crucial means for solving the problems in building communism."[3] The Soviet government took vigorous steps to diminish the importance and usefulness of the other languages in the USSR. After the second occupation of Latvia at the end of World War II, intensive instructions in the Russian language became mandatory in the primary and secondary schools. The Party devoted particular attention to the teaching of Russian in kindergartens. It assigned high priority to the training of kindergarten teachers in methods that would effectively introduce the Russian language at the pre-school level, the optimum age for learning foreign languages. A mix of Russian and non-Russian children provided the best environment for rapid acquisition of spoken Russian. Games would be conducted in Russian, with Russian children acting as leaders and facilitators. Before patriotic holidays, children would memorize songs and poems in Russian. Activities such as "Let's talk about animals in Russian" were interspersed throughout a kindergarten week. The Party did not spare resources for preparing tapes, videos, games, and masks as aids in teaching Russian to the very young.[4]

In universities, Russian soon became the second language of instruction. The local faculty members, invariably trained outside the USSR, could not come up with instructors for the newly designated mandatory subjects of Marxism-Leninism, dialectical materialism, and military science. Most of the growing number of professors imported from Russia spoke no Latvian. Ultimately education at all levels followed two paths: One could attend a Latvian-language or Russian-language elementary school, high school, and university. Government positions started to fill with Russian immigrants, and in the larger cities public business came to be conducted in Russian. A social rule at work, enforced loosely or strictly according to the zeal of the management, prescribed that if any group had at least one member who did not speak Latvian, the group, no matter how large, must converse in Russian. The analogue that if at least one member did not speak Russian the group should use the Latvian language was regarded as both absurd and subversive. In the 1960s, the Latvian communist party's newspaper *Cīņa* (The Struggle) started to publish articles under the heading "Russian Is Not a Foreign Language."[5]

History had to be rewritten in the Soviet mode, exalting Russian and minimizing non-Russian achievements. The Russian people had bequeathed progress to the others. In the revised Baltic histories, the years of independence merited hardly a page. Soviet historians unearthed noted Latvian communists, and the authorities put them on pedestals, literally. Statues of dead communists, most of them killed during Stalin's great purges in 1936 to 1938, filled the Communard Park in Riga, and still more statues could be found in other parks as well. One wonders how many school children making Soviet youth organizations' sponsored pilgrimages to the Communard Park noticed that most of the great men had died in 1937. What did the youth leaders and teachers say? Could Stalin's purges be explained away without wounding the Communist party?

Many buildings bore plaques inscribed in both Latvian and Russian, telling the passersby that some worthy member of the communist party had once occupied a part of the premises. Streets were renamed, in Latvian and Russian, after Soviet dignitaries: Lenin, Kirov, Gorky, and others less well known. The Aristide Briand street, named after the lapsed socialist, the eleven-times premier of France and a recipient of the Nobel peace prize, was renamed after a more congenial Frenchman, Henry Barbusse, whose intellectual journey led him from nationalism to pacifism to militant communism and who died in the Soviet Union. The names of the administrative divisions of Riga, the capital of the Latvian Soviet Republic, bore no Latvian names. The six districts were Kirov, Lenin, Leningrad, Moscow, October, and Proletarian.

The authorities outlawed all national and religious holidays. But working men and women like extra days off; consequently the traditional celebrations of "old superstitions and delusions" were replaced with an allegedly more meaningful set of Soviet holidays: October Revolution Day, International Women's Day, May Day, Victory in the Great Patriotic War Day, and the USSR Constitution Day. Stalin's birthday, once an absolutely splendiferous holiday, disappeared from Soviet calendars in the late 1950s. For children, New Year's Day and Father Frost replaced Christmas and Santa Claus.

Youngsters did receive the official information that the first New Year's tree had been lit by none other than Comrade Lenin for children in the Kremlin.[6]

All movies were distributed directly from Moscow, but every play produced locally had to be approved by the authorities. It was relatively easy to get approval for a Russian play, somewhat more difficult for a Latvian play, and quite difficult for a Western play. Censors vigilantly protected newspapers, magazines, and published books from the contagious germs of nationalism. They had greater difficulties in detecting the virulent strains of nationalism in ballet, music, and painting. For the sake of ideological safety, censors always gave preference to the classics over contemporary works and styles.

All textbooks had to carry the official imprimatur, and consequently there were very few of them. Course outlines in universities came directly from Moscow, and rectors and deans had to make sure that individual instructors closely followed the official outlines. Such regimentation damaged the quality of teaching in the USSR.

After World War II, a number of national monuments were blown up, and the militia and the secret police kept watching the others. People who attempted to place flowers at those monuments were either arrested or had their names registered in the KGB files of the potentially subversive. The displaying or even the possession of the crimson-white-crimson Latvian flag and the singing of the national anthem were punishable by incarceration.

After the declaration of the Latvian independence, the former KGB officers eagerly sought interviews with journalists and displayed a worldwise attitude toward the old repressions. Instead of the stern Stalinist image that had served them so well for two and a half generations, they conveyed very humane feelings about their former rules and regulations. They had always expected some demonstration during the outlawed national holidays, usually nothing more than somebody laying flowers on a forbidden grave or raising the Latvian flag on a chimney, in a park, or in a forest. People who could be expected to do such things were, on the eve of the holiday, committed to psychiatric hospitals for a prophylactic rest cure, but there were always others who put up national flags. On orders from Moscow, high-ranking KGB officers personally had to rush from place to place pulling them down. All this, acknowledged the former KGB officers, was a waste of valuable time because the offense, after all, was not a serious one. Also, while pulling down illegal flags, KGB officers were unable to perform more important tasks. Upon questioning by journalists, the more important tasks turned out to be fighting crime, not at all surveillance of politically dubious persons.

A bizarre peculiarity of the Soviet ideology, far more monarchistic than socialistic in character, was the demand for unreserved adulation and worship of the leader, the General Secretary of the Communist party. His vision and his leadership reached everybody—meant quite literally—through the great Russian people. Whatever words the party leadership demanded, the rank and file supplied with vengeance. The following is an excerpt from the editorial in the leading literary journal in Latvia, *Literatūra un māksla* (Literature and Art), dated July 25, 1948. The translation is mine.

To the great leader of all nations (plural!), our teacher and friend, Joseph Vissarionovich Stalin. . . . Dear and beloved Comrade Stalin . . . for years we dreamed that we shall walk hand in hand with the great Russian people. . . . You inspire us to heroic work and the realization of your great plans. . . . Men have composed many songs but none are loftier than those that are born today. They come from the depths of our hearts and their lyrics address you, the creator of our happiness. . . . You, dear Joseph Vissarionovich, are our cognition, our honor, and our conscience. This is the reason why we mention your name with such love. . . . Let our words carry to you our love and infinite gratitude.

Utterly mindless panegyrics were repeated again and again by all public speakers, most journalists, and many writers. The poet laureate of the Latvian Soviet Republic, Jānis Sudrabkalns, exulted, "Stalin, you savior of nations, you are the father of Latvians to whom the Soviet people are brothers. . . . Everything that is noble and beautiful has been preserved in Moscow."[7] Leaders of lower rank reflected the dazzling light emanating from the Kremlin.

Stalin's successors did not demand the same ardor, but the difference was more of degree than kind. Sharaf R. Rashidov, First Secretary of the Uzbek communist party, characterized Leonid Brezhnev during the Twenty-fifth Congress of the CPSU in 1976 as a man with "supreme modesty, brilliant talents, revolutionary optimism, proletarian solidarity, firm class position, spiritual beauty and personal charm." "The thinkers of the East say: 'When a state is headed by a wise man who loves his people and is concerned about improving his country's lot, this is great happiness for the state and for the people.' The Soviet people . . . call [Brezhnev] such a person."[8] As soon as the Central Committee elected a new General Secretary of the Communist party, he automatically and immediately became the embodiment of supreme wisdom, unique perception, and absolute mastery of Marxism-Leninism. The state publishing house hastened to print his collected works, which, it is safe to assume, nobody read except for those who had to translate them from Russian into the major languages of the Soviet Union. This practice ended with Gorbachev.

Unreserved admiration carried with it the danger of serious embarrassment if someday its object would turn out to be politically incorrect. In time, a number of supreme Soviet leaders became unmentionable (Stalin), nonpersons (Khrushchev), or acknowledged stagnationists (Brezhnev). Stalin's demise necessitated renaming of numerous geographic features. The highest mountain in the USSR, once enthusiastically named "Stalin's Peak," became "Communism Peak." Giving new names inconspicuously to thousands of Stalin streets, boulevards, prospects, and parks caused great headaches to the authorities. Sometimes a city named after Stalin or one of his closest associates regained its former, non-Russian name. Stalinbad, the capital of Tajikistan, became Dushanbe again.

The descent of Stalin's successors did not cause cartographic revolutions, but tons of volumes of collected works had to be recycled. The sharp reversals of certain exalted leaders' reputations damaged the Party's credibility a little, and the weakening of the center in Moscow strengthened somewhat the periphery in Tallin, Riga, Vilnius, and Dushanbe.

Russification made the greatest headway at the workplace. In all fifteen Soviet republics, fourteen of them non-Russian, nobody occupied a high position unless he or she was a Russian or spoke fluent Russian. After World War II, the Baltic Republics underwent forced and intensive industrialization, in which the necessary labor force arrived from Russia, the Ukraine, or Byelorussia. Most of these immigrants settled in the larger cities, in all of which the native population became a minority. Latvians did constitute the majority in rural districts and small towns.[9] Upon retirement, Soviet military officers could settle anywhere in the USSR, and the state guaranteed them apartments without the usual waiting period.[10] All military officers had to be party members, and the Party created second careers for them, usually in the military-industrial complex or in education. Latvian officials, even before independence, asserted that a disproportionate number of military retirees had settled in Latvia, also in Estonia.

Since the bulk of the industrial labor force spoke only Russian, managerial positions required mastery of the Russian language. Early in the fall of 1991, I examined eight major industrial enterprises in the vicinity of Riga. All eight directors were Russians. Some of the engineers and managers were Latvians and spoke in Latvian to me but not to one another. It was evident that I had come upon places of Russian language and culture. A small technical library at an electronics plant had only Russian publications and nothing at all in any other language.

Fluency in the Russian language was a necessity for making a career in industry, but being Russian was preferable. The Party regarded all non-Russians as potentially unreliable. The Balts could not be authorized to go to sea, for they might defect. As a result, hardly any Latvian sailors or officers served in their own republic's fleet of ninety ocean-going vessels.[11] Ethnic Estonians were barred from employment at the Sillamae uranium processing plant in Estonia.[12]

The government and the Supreme Soviet of the Latvian Soviet Socialistic Republic as well as the Central Committee of the Latvian Communist party consisted of both Latvians and Russians. The Latvian members who got into serious trouble had pushed the use of Latvian language, suggesting, for example, that employees of banks serving Latvian clientele should speak Latvian. Moscow regarded national communists as dangerous heretics who must be extirpated by means of dismissals and exile. Khrushchev purged over 1000 Latvian communist party members for alleged "bourgeois-nationalistic" tendencies.

Moscow entrusted the task of watching high-ranking non-Russian communists in each Soviet republic to the Second Secretary of the Republican Communist party and to the Deputy Commander of the local KGB. Both of these positions were reserved for Russians.[13] Even though natives of the Soviet Republics occupied most of the highest positions in their republics, above them loomed a still higher tier of officialdom in Moscow composed either of ethnic Russians or of people Russianized to such a degree that they barely spoke their ostensibly native languages.

IV

The Latvian response to Russification and the frenzied suppression of nationalism by the Soviet authorities took many forms—timid protests at first, bold denunciation near the end of the USSR. It all began in cemeteries.

Latvians traditionally expend much loving care on the family burial plots. This is not a job to be relegated to cemetery maintenance organizations. Families themselves keep the plots neatly raked. Diligently tended flowers, ornamental shrubs, and ground covers beautify the low rectangular mounds that delineate the graves of the departed. Those who can afford it put up tombstones or commission monuments, thus giving employment to sculptors. Well-known monuments mark the graves of popular poets, writers, artists, actors, politicians, and teachers. The cemetery is a place to visit and to memorialize the dead by leaving fresh flowers on their graves. On the annual Memorial Day in November, almost everybody makes a pilgrimage to a cemetery and leaves lighted candles on those graves that mean something to the pilgrim.

Cemeteries quickly evolved into sites for national demonstrations. Piles of cut flowers and a carpet of lighted candles on Memorial Day covered the graves of those who had enriched Latvian culture, sought political independence, or fought foreign oppressors. Many of them the Soviets had classified as former "enemies of the people."

The Soviet authorities realized that cemeteries had turned subversive, but they could not forbid burials and cemetery visits. As a partial solution, they joined the practice of honoring the dead. Distinguished communists and Red Army officers were buried with great pomp near, or next to, Latvian cultural, political, and military heroes, and the communist party workers made sure that fresh and red flowers always ornamented these graves. The two different alphabets used side by side illustrated another small clash of cultures. The Russian tombstones were inscribed in Cyrillic letters, the Latvian tombstones in Latin letters.

The militia and secret police agents kept people away only from some Latvian military cemeteries, the very imposing grave sites of two former presidents in the Forest Cemetery in Riga, and a few other graves of nationalistic significance. But enforcing the proscription, however limited, required a perpetual militia presence in certain cemeteries. It struck an observer as odd to see manned militia sentry boxes and observation posts among graves and crosses. The militiamen seemed to be smoking incessantly.

Baltic cultures venerate the song. During the years of oppression, poets and orators assert, songs vitalize hope and keep alive the vision of unity and freedom. Choral singing became the first national movement in the present Baltic States starting around 1820. At the next stage of development came periodic song festivals, in which members of numerous choruses in the country came together for a mammoth concert. The first Latvia-wide song festival took place in 1873, when over 1000 singers from about forty-five choruses sang, for the first time, the prayer that was to become the national anthem. Between 10,000 and 20,000 singers used to take part in the Estonian and Latvian song festivals in the 1930s.[14]

Initially after World War II, the Soviet authorities forbade all song festivals. But the tradition was deeply ingrained and the authorities themselves wanted to restore normalcy. Therefore, the organizers of song festivals soon received the necessary authorization. The repertoire had to include a mandatory number of Russian songs. The national anthem and certain nationalistic songs were forbidden, but there existed a large number of other songs with nationalistic overtones. In some cases the censors, unable to understand all the nuances of the lyrics, let certain songs slip through, whereas the audience appreciated fully the nationalistic and anti-Soviet implications. In general, writers, poets, editors, choir masters, and theater directors became very adept at fooling the censors while the public became very adept at reading between the lines.

Many Westerners have marveled at the popularity of poets in Eastern Europe and the USSR, where poetry readings used to attract audiences in thousands. Every Soviet republic celebrated Poets' Day, when poets visited schools in the mornings and read their works in public squares or in front of monuments of popular writers in the afternoons. The popularity of poets did not rest entirely or even largely on literary merit. When the press is shackled by censorship and journalists mouth the party line, the public looks for truth in literature and eagerly reads between the lines. Under Russification and totalitarianism, the paramount role of the artist was to keep the spirit of nationalism alive and to depict the true conditions of life in face of official lying. The authorities, of course, knew this, and from time to time prison camps, the Gulag archipelago, sucked in recalcitrant men and women of letters and the arts.

In the West, no poet earns similar adulation. When editorials openly lambast the administration, nobody needs to read between the lines. In repressed countries, poets and writers become leaders of society not by choice or leadership ability but by virtue of being perceived as the only truthful and honest men and women. The Party had power, but the persistent lying by its officials had eroded its moral authority. Vaclav Havel, the playwright, political prisoner, leader of the resistance movement, and, finally, president of the Czech Republic, wrote that "if someone spends his life writing the truth without caring for consequences, he inevitably becomes a political authority in a totalitarian regime."[15] In the Baltic States, the closest parallel to Vaclav Havel is Vytautas Landsbergis, a professor of musicology, who became the first president of independent Lithuania.

The Soviet authorities had success in their campaign against religion. Under persecution and denial of resources, the major religious bodies lost any role in charity and ethics. Houses of worship gradually emptied of all but the hard core of the fervently faithful. The major exception in the western USSR was Lithuania, where no repressive measures succeeded in wresting the population away from the Roman Catholic church. Despite the arrests of some of its editors and publishers, the clandestine *The Chronicle of the Lithuanian Catholic Church* survived between 1972 and 1990 as the only continuous underground publication (*samizdat*) in the USSR. Primarily it documented human rights violations in Lithuania.

The displacement of religion created a spiritual void that communism, despite its shrines, all-embracing ideology, and pomp failed to fill. In the non-Russian USSR, it was nationalism with its symbols, songs, heroes, and ideas that served as a substitute for religion. It can be argued that the fervent Catholicism in Lithuania and Poland was far more a nationalistic than a religious expression. In Riga, newlyweds had their pictures taken in front of the Monument of Freedom erected during the period of Latvian independence. Wedding feasts rarely passed without the singing of nationalistic songs. The flowers in cemeteries, the literature and arts (open to nationalistic interpretation), the *samizdat*, the forbidden songs at private parties, and the growing number of various folklore groups kept the coals of nationalism smoldering. The worldwide ecology movement took a nationalistic form in the Baltic Republics. It condemned the pollution of the Baltic Sea by the Soviet nuclear and nonnuclear navy, and the degradation of land, air, and water by heavy industry controlled from Moscow that practiced no environmental protection policies. The only halfway affective measure against nationalism was intermarriage. When Latvians, or Ukrainians, or Byelorussians, or many other nationalities married Russians, the Russian side prevailed and dominated perhaps one-half of the time. Intermarriage was exceedingly rare between Russians and Muslims from the Soviet Central Asian Republics. *Shariat*, the Muslim law against misalliance, was probably the main reason why very few Muslim girls married Russians. Every year a number of Muslim men used to return home from military service accompanied by Russian wives. However, when Muslim men marry Russian women, the children almost always select their father's nationality.[16]

In the three Baltic Republics, living memory of their independence between the two world wars never died because the period was too recent. The numerous Baltic social, political, and religious organizations in the West set as their paramount goal the liberation of the Baltic States from Soviet occupation. Constant lobbying kept reminding Western governments and media of the strivings for independence in the Soviet Baltic Republics. But as the events after the August putsch showed, nationalism was perhaps unexpectedly strong among the other nationalities in the USSR as well. Before 1991 had ended, all former Soviet Republics had declared their independence.

V

To many nationalities in the former USSR, history has bequeathed a heavy burden. Centuries-long unsettled territorial disputes keep on souring relations between neighboring ethnic groups. Past wars all too often ended in defeat followed by lengthy periods of enslavement or subjugation and cultural or religious degradation. Even worse, some nationalities passed through many centuries as a mass of nameless peasants with no manifest history of their own. Others were labeled according to their religion. Until the early nineteenth century, Byelorussians, Ukrainians, Lithuanians, and people living in eastern Latvia were known primarily as Catholics. The few periods of national independence never lasted very long, while memories of the perpetrators of past indignities and cruelties linger on from generation to generation.

In one respect history has been kind to the Baltic peoples. Living under centuries-long subjugation by foreign powers, they never went to war with each other or seriously contested a piece of territory. Many other nationalities within the tsarist and subsequently the Soviet empire carried over from past periods serious grudges and grievances against one another, which the Moscow authorities never failed to exploit.

In Transcaucasia, the intermingling in a relatively small area of some eight ethnically, linguistically, and religiously different groups has been a persistent source of conflict. Apart from the Russian influence and rule, the region has been dominated and contested by its three largest nationalities: the Armenians, the Azerbaijanis (Azers), and the Georgians. In Transcaucasia, frontiers twist and turn between high mountain ranges, leaving pockets of one ethnic group inside the territory of another.

The genocide of the Armenians by the Turks between 1895 and 1915 has never been forgotten. The Christian Armenians mistrust the Muslim Azerbaijanis, who are a Turkic people. Since 1988, Armenia and Azerbaijan have been fighting a war or carrying on skirmishes over Nagorno-Karabach, a region inside Azerbaijan that is populated mostly by Armenians. Azerbaijan would not let it go in part because the region holds some of Azerbaijan's national shrines and a sacred forest near which the Azers once defeated the Persians.

Attempted cultural and political domination engenders resistance. Inside Georgia, the Abhazs and Osetians harbor strong anti-Georgian nationalism. In eastern Georgia, Azers outnumber Georgians and desire unification with their mother country. Like the former Yugoslavia, Transcaucasia abounds with ethnic tensions among peoples who take their histories extremely seriously and never forgive or forget anything.

Nationalists in Central Asia in particular referred to Russians as colonialists and the Soviet Union as a colonial power. The Soviet Central Asian nationalities—the Khazakhs, the Uzbeks, the Turkmens, the Tajiks, and the Khirgizs, most of them Muslims—are closely related to the main ethnic groups in Iran, Afghanistan, and China and share their biases and animosities, as well as carry on a few of their own. In 1944, as a punishment for the alleged cooperation with the German army, Stalin deported the Meshketian Turks of Southwest Georgia, the Crimean Tatars, and the Volga Germans to Uzbekistan. The forcibly transplanted ethnic groups could not get along with the much larger native Uzbek population. Persistent tension culminated in the bloody anti-Meshketian riots of 1988. The Soviet government shipped the former deportees back to their home territories, but there, too, they found no welcome among the local Georgians, Ukrainians, and Russians.

When the Soviet government drew up the map of the Central Asian Soviet Republics, it placed the ancient centers of Tajik culture, Bukhara and Samarkand, inside Uzbekistan, and the culturally important Uzbek city of Khojand (since 1936, Leninbad) inside Tajikistan. Occasionally historical claims on each other's territory find vocal expression among Uzbeks and Tajiks.[17] In Tajikistan, as in the neighboring Afghanistan, towering mountain ranges shelter fighters for various causes. Internecine conflicts arise not with different minorities but among different clans (i.e., Tajiks from different regions). The People's Front that won the 1992–93 civil war originated in Leninbad and the Kulyab and Kurgan-Tube regions in the north. The defeated Islam opposition came largely from the Garm-Kartogin and Pamir regions in the south. Many of the Islamic fighters escaped to Afghanistan and, in alliance with the Afghan mujahedin, kept raiding the border regions of Tajikistan.

Ukrainians have been divided among themselves. The western part of the country has bred some of the most rabid nationalist groups anywhere in the former USSR (they are not only anti-Russian but also anti-Polish, anti-Byelorussian, anti-Lithuanian, and anti-other-Ukrainians as well). In the more industrialized and more Russianized eastern Ukraine, the nationalist movement has been more conciliatory toward other ethnic groups, including Russians. Lithuania and Poland have had a running dispute as to which of the two owns Vilnius, the present capital of Lithuania. At the zenith of its power, Lithuania, one of the great medieval empires, ruled over vast territories to the east that extended almost to Moscow. Eventually the Lithuanian state became Polonized and then, together with Poland, was conquered by Tsar Peter the Great. Lithuania declared its independence again on February 16, 1918, with Vilnius as its capital. In October of 1920, Poland occupied Vilnius and kept it until 1939. Lithuanians moved their capital to Kaunas. After occupying the northern part of Poland at the outset of World War II, the Soviets decided in favor of Lithuania. Vilnius became the capital of the Lithuanian Soviet Socialistic Republic and subsequently the capital of the independent Republic of Lithuania. At present, the population of Vilnius is about 55 percent Lithuanian,[18] but the 260,000-strong Polish minority in Lithuania is heavily concentrated in the Vilnius district. Occasionally Lithuanian nationalists have taken an anti-Polish stance fully reciprocated, in turn, by the anti-Lithuanian stance of the Polish minority.

Numerically Russians constituted a minority in every non-Russian republic. Russian, however, was the dominant language in economics and politics of every Soviet republic. Russians held the balance of power and enjoyed apartment and job selection privileges. The indigenous people complained that Russians made them feel like members of minorities in their own republics.

Nationalism either binds an ethnic group closer together against a common, usually stronger, foe, or assumes a comprehensive superiority over other, usually weaker, ethnic or religious groups. Nationalism of the first kind helped to break up the Soviet Union. As the far-flung empire collapsed, Russians suddenly found themselves being a genuine minority in each of the newly independent non-Russian states. Making matters worse for the Russian speakers, the indigenous languages replaced Russian as the official state language.

After independence, the indigenous populations of all former Soviet republics clamored for the reversal of their allegedly second-class status under the tsarist and Soviet empires. The new political leaders, mostly native ex-communists, demonstrated a quickly diminishing loyalty to all things Russian.

The worst fate awaited Russians and other Russian-speaking immigrants in the former Soviet Asian and Caucasus Republics, where the local people did not seem to fear the Red Army. In the Tajik civil war, Russia supported the winning side, but warfare moved back and forth across the country and the losing side vented its rage on Russians. By 1994, some 350,000 Russian civilians out of the 600,000 in 1992 had fled Tajikistan. Some of them settled in the radiation-contaminated zone surrounding the Chernobyl nuclear power plant.[19] Many of the victims of the vicious wars in Armenia, Georgia, and Chechnya were Russian civilians.

In Kazakhstan, where 44 percent of the 1994 population were Russians and other Slavs, Kazakh became the official language even though only one-half of the ethnic Kazakhs could speak it. Most of the Russians live in the cities, but in the rural regions, ethnic Kazakh gangs imparted the knowledge to their Russian neighbors that they were not wanted.

After independence, constitutions and laws of the former Soviet Republics favored their citizens. The new legislators made sure that aliens, mostly Russians, could not obtain citizenship easily. The Baltic Republics do not have a tradition of interethnic violence. However, no Russian who had arrived or was born in Estonia or Latvia after 1940 qualified for automatic citizenship. Naturalization requires passing an examination in the indigenous language. Russian representatives charged that the language requirement was too difficult and effectively disenfranchised hundreds of thousands of Russian speakers.

NOTES

1. Viktors Kalniņš, "Daudznacionālā, bet ne vienotā . . ." (The Multinational but not United . . .), *Latvija šodien 1983* (Latvia Today 1983), p. 109.

2. Rimvydas Šilbajoris, a Lithuanian scholar, quoted in Anatol Lieven, *The Baltic Revolution.* New Haven and London: Yale University Press, 1993, p. 89.

3. Directive of the Central Committee of the Estonian Communist party, December 19, 1978.

4. Uldis Ğērmanis, *Zināšanai: raksti par mūsu un padomju lietām* (For Your Knowledge: Writings about Our and Soviet Matters). Stockholm: Ziemelzvaigzne, 1985, p. 85. Interview with kindergarten teacher Jekatrina Rjabceva, *Sieviete un ğimene* (Woman and the Family), April 1983, reprinted in *Latvija šodien 1983*, p. 116.

5. Kalniņš, p. 109.

6.Viktors Strunskis, "'Padomju cilvēka' ieaugšana sabiedrībā" (The Socialization of the 'Soviet Man'), *Latvija šodien 1983*, p. 121.

7. Māris Rauda, "'Tev, Stāļin, sekojam par lielo cīņu tekām' "('We Follow Thee, Stalin, over the Paths of the Great Struggles: Notes about Jānis Sudrabkalns and His, in 1984 Republished Volume of Poetry, *Brāļu saime* that Earlier Had Won Him the Stalin's Premium'), *Latvija šodien 1985*, pp. 41–42.

8. Edward A. Allworth, *The Modern Uzbeks.* Stanford: Hoover Institution Press, 1990, p. 315.

9. *Statistikas gadagrāmata '89* (Statistical Yearbook for 1989). Latvian State Statistics Committee, 1990, p. 23.

10. David K. Willis, *Klass: How Russians Really Live.* New York: St. Martin's Press, 1975, p. 12.

11. Lieven, p. 97.

12.Will Radecki, "Estonian Town Prefers Russian for Administrative Language." *The Baltic Observer*, June 8–14, 1995, p. 5.

13. Lieven, p. 99.

14. Valentīns Bērzkalns, *Latviešu dziesmu svētku vēsture 1864–1940* (History of Latvian Song Festivals 1864–1940). New York: Grāmatu draugs, 1965, pp. 45 and 339–524.

15. Vaclav Havel, quoted in Bernard Gwertzman and Michael T. Kaufman (eds.), *The Collapse of Communism*. New York: Times Books, 1990, p. 345.

16. Michael Rywkin, *Moscow's Muslim Challenge* (revised ed.). Armonk, N.Y.: M. E. Sharpe, 1990, p. 86.

17. Teresa Rakowska-Harmstone, *Russia and Nationalism in Central Asia, the Case of Tadzikistan*. Baltimore and London: The Johns Hopkins Press, 1970, pp. 179–180. Allworth, p. 303.

18. Lieven, p. 184.

19. *The Wall Street Journal*, November 8, 1995.

4

The Building of a Civil Society, or What the Putschists Wanted to Break Up

The coup occurred because of all the changes that have taken place, and it failed because of all the changes that have taken place.

—William Taubman,
The New York Times, August 21, 1991

I

In the heyday of the Soviet empire, all roads led to Moscow, but by 1991, the seventh year of Gorbachev's rule, many road signs had been reversed and many more were being reversed. The putsch attempted to overthrow Mikhail Gorbachev because his leadership had not stopped the USSR from moving in those directions that led away from central authority.

The public confidence in the basic competence of the Party and the government remained pretty strong until 1986. The authorities supposedly worked responsibly, if not efficiently, and the news media reported events more or less accurately. It was Chernobyl in April of 1986 that "psychologically unhinged" the Soviet Union.[1] The impact of the accident was too large for successful concealment or trivialization. Nobody believed that the blame fell solely on incompetent technicians. High party and government officials had blatantly lied while the delayed and incomplete evacuation jeopardized the health of hundreds of thousands, possibly millions. Ecological protests swept throughout the USSR. The Byelorussian independence movement grew out of communal efforts to help radiation victims, particularly the children. Due to the wind direction during the first week after the accident, the early and heaviest fallout fell largely on the Mogilev district of the Byelorussian Republic. This did not precipitate a mass evacuation, and the media kept silent. Instead of informing and assisting the public, the authorities denied the existence of any serious health hazard.

For the first two months, the official news media gave the accident only minimal coverage. By July the Soviet information policy began to change. The media started to give detailed reports of the Chernobyl clean-up process in the aftermath of the explosion and, for the first time, analyzed the dangers of radiation to the general public. The next dramatic accident occurred on August 31, when a Soviet luxury liner in the Black Sea, the *Admiral Nakhimov*, collided with a freighter and sank with the loss of 398 lives. This time the media spared no details.[2] Journalists kept on testing the limitations put on the freedom of the press and saw that they were rapidly diminishing. Soon no office or official could entirely escape the scrutiny of the media.

It was *glasnost*, Gorbachev's policy of "openness"—essentially the abolishing of censorship—that brought down the Communist party as the undisputed moral and political power in the USSR. Not disenchantment with Marxism but the revulsion against systematic official lying killed communism as a set of moral guideposts and a system of values. The Party could not survive open criticism because its authority rested on lies. It had created an ideological structure that had no basis in reality. Instead, it rested on two clay pillars: the comprehensive falsification of history, and the isolation of the Soviet population from foreign influences and examples. Actually, technology dictated that the Soviet system had to go because it could not have survived the Internet, the instantaneous access to the uncensorable worldwide information network.

The lifting of censorship from history dealt a devastating blow to the Communist party. Nothing at all had happened the way it was described in the official histories and literature. One could argue that the entire Soviet society consisted of only two groups: the small group of the *nomenklatura* as the ruling class and a huge group of economical and political victims, many of them "repressed" victims. The adjective *repressed* meant that a person had been arrested, exiled, sent to labor camps, or executed.

In the process of making history honest, the Baltic Republics played a major role in the USSR. The most damaging document that came to the fore was the Molotov-Ribbentrop Pact of 1939 concerning the three Baltic Republics. The Pact disclosed collaboration between Nazi Germany and the Soviet Union and went a long way toward explaining why the German invasion caught the Soviet Union unprepared and vulnerable. The Party under the leadership of Stalin had acted immorally and, much worse, had made a serious mistake that cost the Soviet people millions of casualties at the beginning of World War II.

According to the Soviet version of history, the former Baltic States had joined the USSR voluntarily in 1940 by a popular vote of well over 95 percent. But the official history concealed a damaging fact that had been formulated with legal precision in the 1939 Soviet-German Non-Aggression Pact. In this document, better known as the Molotov-Ribbentrop Pact, both parties agreed to abstain, individually and in coalition with other states, from any military action against one another. The Pact was signed on August 23, 1939, eight days before Germany invaded Poland. Stalin, believing that Hitler would honor the non-aggression pact, made no serious preparations for war. The German invasion of the Soviet Union in the summer of 1941 completely surprised and routed the Red Army, pushing it back to the gates of Leningrad and Moscow.

The Molotov-Ribbentrop Pact also contained a secret protocol, as amended, in which Stalin and Hitler divided Northeastern, Eastern, and Southeastern Europe between themselves. The three Baltic States and Finland were assigned to the Soviet sphere of influence, while Poland was split roughly in half. Germany declared its complete disinterestedness in Besarabia and Southeastern Europe. The document surfaced during the Nuremberg trial of Nazi officials. The Soviet government was able to suppress its publication, but the knowledge of it spread and eventually seeped into the USSR.[3]

The Molotov-Ribbentrop Pact supported some other facts that belied the official pronouncements that the Baltic States had joined the USSR as an expression of popular will. The Red Army had, in fact, simultaneously occupied Estonia, Latvia, and Lithuania on June 17, 1940, and in each country, the Soviet-sponsored elections had only one slate of candidates.

The Soviet government concealed the Molotov-Ribbentrop Pact for almost fifty years. Gorbachev mentioned it in one of his speeches, critical of Stalin, in 1987, but the break came during August of 1988 when the text of the secret protocol was published in the legal press, not just *samizdat*, of all three Baltic Republics. The Soviet government at first "could not locate" the secret protocols. One year later, in the summer of 1989, the Supreme Soviet in Moscow acknowledged the existence of the Molotov-Ribbentrop Pact with all its secret protocols. The Pact implied the illegitimacy of the Soviet rule over the Baltic Republics.[4]

Baltic independence movements made effective use of the Molotov-Ribbentrop Pact in showing the Soviets as occupiers and colonialists. A spectacular demonstration took place on August 23, 1989. Perhaps as many as 2 million Estonians, Latvians, and Lithuanians joined hands in a human chain stretching from Tallin, the capital of Estonia, to Vilnius, the capital of Lithuania, for a distance of some 380 miles. This event attracted wide coverage by the Western media and acid denunciations of the Baltic "virus of nationalism" from Moscow.

II

The combination of the success of *glasnost* with the failure of *perestroika* created the conditions for breaking up the Soviet system. After 1985 for the first time since Lenin's New Economic Policy (NEP) of the early 1920s, high party officials openly acknowledged that the economy was performing poorly and getting worse. At this time, no major Western power favored the breaking up of the USSR. The most popular statesman in the world was Mikhail Gorbachev. The Soviet and Western hope for a more prosperous and secure future rested on *perestroika*, the restructuring of the Soviet economy, where sharply reduced central planning would coexist with a free market driven by profit-motivated private enterprises. The promising and planning of economic reforms went on continuously, but the implementation lagged far behind. Gorbachev had difficulties accepting decisive ideological breaks with the past, such as privatization of industry and decollectivization of agriculture. Comprehensive radical plans invariably ended up as watered-down versions that did not remove much power from the center in Moscow.

The economic reforms did not change everyday life for most Soviet citizens. As late as 1991, the overwhelming majority still worked for state enterprises. The central plan had been replaced by government purchases planned in Moscow. As a result, industry continued working primarily for the government. People bought most of their goods and services from the state stores and service establishments, paying government-controlled prices. One had to search far and wide for private restaurants, usually thought to be the first object of privatization. None of the few private restaurants that I saw appeared to be particularly successful. A number of cooperatives had been established in every sector of the economy. All of them were allegedly "greedy," a Soviet term for "profit-motivated." It was very difficult to discover any difference between state enterprises and cooperatives because as an enterprise converted itself into a cooperative, the director remained the same.

In February of 1989, the USSR had 200 joint ventures with foreigners; China had about 10,000.[5] Many foreign businesspeople scouted out the potentially huge Soviet market, but very few were willing to invest significant resources in a command economy that had no clear future direction. A few joint ventures foundered on the rocks of Soviet rules and practices, primarily the absence of a legal framework for doing business. Stalin might be dead, but his rule that an official's word is the law was very much alive.[6]

Perestroika failed to fulfill its original promise to bring "a new quality to the socialist way of life."[7] It did not raise the standard of living and did not boost the growth rate of the Soviet economy. It did restructure the management of the economy by giving individual republics greater economic autonomy.

On July 26, 1989, after a spirited discussion, the USSR Supreme Soviet in Moscow gave all three Baltic Republics the right of self-financing starting on January 1, 1990. For Gorbachev this constituted a significant experiment for *perestroika*. If it worked in the Baltic Republics, it might work in the other republics as well. Gorbachev picked the Baltic Republics for experimentation because they showed the highest labor productivity and had the highest per capita incomes in the USSR. The opponents argued that self-financing would make Russia a raw-materials-supplying colony of the Baltics; others saw in it a thinly disguised shift toward political independence. Nonetheless, the legislation passed with 412 votes for, 15 against, and 155 abstentions.[8]

Self-financing meant that the Baltic Republics would have to balance their own budgets and for that purpose would be allowed to keep about one-half of their tax revenues. The All-Union five-year plan remained binding, but certain industries (agriculture, food production, retailing, social services, and light industry) came under republic jurisdiction. The Republics would also gain some say in foreign trade and would be allowed to enter into joint ventures with foreigners. On the balance, about 60 percent of all enterprises would come under republic control, while 40 percent—the larger ones—remained under the control of the All-Union ministries in

Moscow. The USSR Supreme Soviet expanded the self-financing to a level of almost complete economic autonomy on November 27, 1989, this time by a single vote. The independence movements did not think that the legislation went far enough in the direction of sovereignty.

III

The Baltic independence movements of the late 1980s focused on three main themes: the public disclosure and discussion of the Molotov-Ribbentrop Pact, the depredation of the environment, and the forced Russification and Russian immigration that threatened to reduce the indigenous populations, especially Latvians, to dwindling minorities in their own republics. Even communist party members could show concern over such issues without abjuring the Party. The hardened veterans of the Great Patriotic War and Stalin era, as they grudgingly approached retirement, complained that the new *nomenklatura* all too readily yielded to foreign influences and permitted ideological compromises.

In 1988, all three Baltic Republics saw the formation of highly visible pro-independence umbrella movements called Popular Fronts in Estonia and Latvia, and *Sajudis* in Lithuania. All three organizations attracted many communist party members. The original name of *Sajudis* was "The Movement (i.e., *Sajudis*) for *Perestroika* in Lithuania." In Estonia, one of the founders of the Popular Front , the National Independence Party, had emerged from an earlier political organization called "The Group for the Disclosure of the Molotov-Ribbentrop Pact."[9]

The Baltic Popular Fronts and *Sajudis* quickly gained considerable reputation. The nascent independence movements in the other non-Russian republics held them up as an example of what can be accomplished. The Popular Fronts and *Sajudis* cooperated with similar groups in the Ukraine, Armenia, Georgia, Moldavia, and among the Crimean Tatars. Early in 1990, the Latvian Popular Front successfully mediated the armed conflict between the Armenians and Azerbaijanis over the Nagorno-Karabach region. The peace talks in Latvia did not resolve the basic dispute, but hostilities ceased for a while.

With the help of the *Sajudis*, Byelorussians formed a Popular Front in June of 1989 in Vilnius. When the correspondent to the *Moscow News* asked the Byelorussians why they had gone abroad to form a national movement, the reply was that the reactionary authorities at home would not permit it.[10]

The Soviet political establishment started to change from within. In every republic, members of the indigenous population held the majority of seats in the Supreme Soviet, the republic's parliament. Ordinarily the ostensibly supreme legislative body exercised little initiative, working primarily through its committees, which reviewed bills submitted by the council of ministers. Once a bill reached the floor of the Supreme Soviet, the deputies typically rubber-stamped it.

In 1988 and 1989, the Supreme Soviets of Estonia, Latvia, and Lithuania, each with a clear communist party majority, started to pass legislation that mirrored the aspirations of the independence movements. The Supreme Soviets of the Baltic Republics voted to make Estonian, Latvian, and Lithuanian their respective state's language. They also restored the legality of the national flags, anthems, and coats of arms. Due to a new emphasis on religious freedom, the surveillance of religious activities tapered off, and in 1988 Christmas came to be celebrated openly again. The KGB, habituated to hunting down the singers of forbidden songs and the keepers of anti-Soviet symbols, lost a large part of its workload.

On November 16, 1988, the Estonian Supreme Soviet adopted a resolution of sovereignty whereby in Estonian territory, Estonian laws took precedence over Soviet laws and all Estonian natural resources became the Republic's own property. On November 26, the Presidium of the Supreme Soviet of the USSR in Moscow declared the Estonian decision invalid. On December 7, the Estonian Supreme Soviet reaffirmed its November 16 decision and reasserted its right to override All-Union laws that infringe on local autonomy.

The regularly scheduled elections of the People's Deputies to the USSR Supreme Soviet took place in March of 1989. The results presaged radical changes in Soviet politics. Many senior communist party officials lost to relative newcomers in Moscow, Leningrad, Kiev, Lvov, Yaroslav, Tomsk, and other cities and regions. In the Baltic Republics, the elections ended with the Popular Fronts' and *Sajudis* majorities. In Moscow, Boris Yeltsin won with 89 percent of the votes cast over a candidate backed by the local party machine.[11] However, these were still one-party elections. The winners as well as the losers were members of the Communist party.

A more serious development for the future of the USSR was the splintering of the monolithic Communist Party of the Soviet Union (CPSU) into independent republican communist parties, first in

Lithuania in 1989 and then in Estonia and Latvia in 1990. Contemporaneously, many members resigned from the Communist party. By one estimate, the Party lost one-fifth of its 20 million members.[12] As a major change, the Central Committee agreed to surrender the CPSU monopoly on political power on February 7, 1990.[13]

The next election took place in February and March of 1990, when each Soviet republic elected a new Supreme Soviet. In the Baltic Republics, in the first multiparty elections in the USSR, the communists lost their majorities and the new parliaments set as their main task the restoration of independence.

Lithuania acted first. By the Act of March 11, 1990, the new Supreme Soviet proclaimed the restoration of the independent Republic of Lithuania. The new Republic sought in vain immediate diplomatic recognition in the West.

Estonia moved toward full independence more cautiously. On March 30, 1990, the Estonian Supreme Soviet ruled the Soviet power in Estonia to be illegal and declared a transition period for the restoration of the Republic of Estonia.

Latvia acted last, but finally, on May 4, 1990, its Supreme Soviet adopted "The Declaration of the Renewal of the Independence of the Republic of Latvia" and declared a transition period to a full sovereignty. As a sign of a new era, the Supreme Soviet, a Russian term, became the Supreme Council.

IV

By the summer of 1990, of the three Baltic Republics only Lithuania had declared itself to be a completely independent and sovereign country, but the other two, Estonia and Latvia, acted as if they, too, were independent and sovereign. Their Supreme Councils hastened to replace Soviet laws with new ones patterned either after the legislation of the European Community or the laws of the independence period before the Soviet occupation. The new laws restored private property and legalized the process of breaking up and privatizing state enterprises. Newly appointed foreign ministers traveled to the West as semiofficial guests of Western governments. Foreign economic relations took the form of joint ventures, while a steadily increasing number of foreign businesspeople arrived in Tallin, Riga, Vilnius, and beyond. Very soon the only areas restricted to foreigners were the Soviet military installations. Another sign of considerable independence from Moscow was the influx of numerous

Western consultants. Perhaps the majority were men and women of Baltic origin, but a large minority had no ethnic ties to the region. Irrespective of their fields of expertise, all Western consultants had one paramount objective: to help dismantle the Soviet system.

Nobody had the occupation of censor any longer, and one of the most popular topics for the media was unmasking the outrages and inhumanities of the Soviet regime. The press paid a great deal of attention to the sad plight of conscripts in the Soviet armed forces. Officers and the senior noncommissioned officers blatantly terrorized and brutalized conscripts and the junior enlisted men. In particular, they picked on men from the Baltic and the Central Asian Republics. Many deaths had resulted. Since the beginnings of the Soviet state, criticism of the Red Army, Navy, and Air Force had been a taboo. The "honor of the uniform" had to be defended always by silencing critics. Now the government's own investigating committees, appointed by Gorbachev for the USSR and by Yeltsin for the Russian Republic, revealed that between 1985 and 1990, an estimated 15,000 conscripts had died from "non-combat causes," about 3000 more than were killed in the Afghan War.[14] All three Baltic governments tried to get the authorization from Moscow that conscripts from the Baltic Republics would be permitted to serve out their terms of service in the Baltic Republics. The authorities, caught between the Red Army and organizations like the increasingly vociferous Mothers of Russian Soldiers, vacillated.

National flags, anthems, and symbols occupied a place of honor again. Churches and synagogues started to fill up with slightly embarrassed worshipers, who were unaccustomed to religious ritual. When do we stand up? Sit down? However, the obtrusive Soviet military presence served as a poignant reminder that Moscow did not regard the Baltic Republics as independent and sovereign. The Communist party, too, held fast to its symbols, controlled the major newspapers, and owned the newest and best buildings in every city, town, and village. And as an old slogan used to say, the KGB never slept.

The communist counterparts to the pro-independence Popular Fronts and the *Sajudis* were the Intermovement in Estonia, the International Front (Interfront) in Latvia, and the *Yedinstvo* (Unity) in Lithuania. These organizations, consisting mostly of the CPSU members, acted as the opposition in parliaments and, with palpable support from Moscow and the military, opposed radical economic reforms and stood in readiness to take over the reins of government.

Gorbachev categorically opposed republic secession from the USSR. On April 18, 1990, about one month after the Lithuanian declaration of independence, the Soviet government initiated a partial economic and political blockade by cutting off the supply of crude oil to Lithuanian refineries and by sharply reducing the supply of natural gas. The authorities also blocked railway transport of certain goods to Lithuania, and the Soviet border guards turned back all foreigners seeking entry into Lithuania.

The effects of the blockade raised the Lithuanian official unemployment rate from virtually zero to about 3 percent. But in the interlocking economy of the USSR, Lithuania could retaliate by curtailing exports to the other republics, particularly shipments of food to Leningrad. Instead of breaking the Lithuanian resolve, the blockade stimulated worldwide sympathy for Lithuania and created new shortages of goods in the USSR. Both sides sought a compromise and found it. The Lithuanian government, following a joint recommendation of French president Mitterand and German chancellor Kohl, declared a temporary moratorium on the Declaration of Independence, and on June 30 Gorbachev lifted the unpopular blockade.

Gorbachev's attempts to keep the empire together did not damage his reputation in the West, but inside the USSR, the various ethnic groups struggling for either independence or autonomy perceived Gorbachev as an enemy. The Gorbachev-sponsored law on secession made seceding from the Union virtually impossible. Secession required a two-thirds vote in a popular referendum followed by a five-year period during which the seceding republic would negotiate individual secession agreements with each of the other Soviet Republics. After all this, the USSR Supreme Soviet still had to ratify the secession. A 10 percent vote by the population could stop the process at any time and force a new referendum. Moreover, the seceding republic had to pay the resettlement costs for all of those who wished to remain in the USSR.[15] Very clearly, the law intended to keep the republics in the Union.

At the same time, the Soviet and Western media reported that radical economic changes were occurring in the Baltic Republics that embraced both nationalism and capitalism. By the end of the year, Gorbachev's patience had worn thin, and 1991 began with an ugly period, known in all three Baltic Republics as "the January days."

V

During January of 1991, the Kremlin attempted to squash by force of arms the independent statehood of Lithuania and to terminate the transition period to full independence in Latvia. Of the three Baltic Republics, Latvia had the largest Russian minority, which, it was generally believed, would support a policy of squelching movements that aimed at secession from the USSR. Nevertheless, the bloodshed started in Lithuania, which had been since the March 11, 1990 declaration of independence a particularly sharp thorn in Moscow's side. The authorities in the Kremlin assumed that once the independence movements fell before the Red Army in Lithuania and Latvia, Estonians would give in without any application of force.

The Kremlin adopted the same tactics that had legitimized the use of military force in East Germany and Hungary in the 1950s and in Czechoslovakia in 1968. The Moscow-controlled media alleged that the local governments had surrendered control over the situation to subversive fascist groups and that the true representatives or workers and peasants (i.e., the local communist parties) called upon the Red Army for help in restoring order and socialism.

In Lithuania, the protagonists were the elected government led by the chairman of the Supreme Council, Vytautas Landsbergis, on one side and a mysterious Lithuania's Salvation Committee on the other. The Committee arose from the mostly Russian *Yedinstvo* movement, but the names of the Committee's leaders were never announced. The majority of the population supported the Landsbergis' government, while the Communist party, aided by the Red Army, backed the Salvation Committee.

In Latvia, the protagonists were the elected government led by Ivars Godmanis, the chairman of the Council of Ministers, and Anatolijs Gorbunovs, the chairman of the Supreme Council, on one side and the Interfront's People's Salvation Committee on the other. One of its co-chairmen was Alfreds Rubiks, first secretary of the Latvian Communist party. As in Lithuania, the Soviet authorities championed the Salvation Committee.

The first serious incident in the Baltics occurred on January 2, when the special troops of the Soviet Interior Ministry, the Black Berets (or OMON), occupied the Press Center building in Riga, which housed the printing plant and the editorial offices of most Latvian newspapers and magazines. The troops not only barred the deputy chairman of the Latvian Supreme Council and the deputy chairman of the Council of Ministers from entering the building but jabbed them with the barrels of submachine guns. A clear signal had been sent to the Latvian government that its vaunted sovereignty and control over its territory were a mirage.

People had given the name Black Berets to the Militia Units for Special Missions, also known as Special Militia or by their Russian acronym, OMON. These units were formed in 1988 throughout the Soviet Union from volunteers who could pass a rigorous physical examination and a political reliability test. Intensive physical and hand-to-hand combat training distinguished OMON from other militia units. It was said that many OMON members had seen service in Afghanistan.

OMON units reported directly to the USSR Minister of Interior in Moscow and could be employed by local authorities only with the Minister's authorization. Their loyalty to the Party was unconditional. In Riga, they formed a cooperative, the Viking, which, for a fee, undertook to provide security for CPSU buildings and property. Mr. Aloizs Vaznis, the Minister of Interior for the Latvian Soviet Republic during the period May 1990 to August 1991, described them as fanatics who follow orders and do not think independently. In an interview given to *Rīgas balss* (Riga's Voice), the afternoon newspaper of Riga, Mr. Vaznis counseled the public: "I think that we should treat them as mentally sick people: calmly and with respect, always keeping in mind their sickness."[16] Earlier the Minister had requested in vain that OMON be removed from Latvia.

In Lithuania, a large number of additional Soviet troops arrived during the first seven days of January, ostensibly to enforce conscription laws and to apprehend deserters. Their arrivals coincided with a severe governmental crisis in Lithuania. During the New Year's break, the prime minister, Kazmiera Prunskiene, had announced cuts in subsidies and a 320 percent price increase for basic foodstuffs. Wage and salary increases somewhat assuaged these measures. On January 8, when the Supreme Council assembled for the first time in the new year, the *Yedinstvo* had organized a demonstration, some 2000 strong, outside the parliament building. It protested the price hike and demanded the dissolution of the Supreme Council and the resignation of the cabinet. About thirty demonstrators had to be forcibly ejected from the parliament building. The Lithuanian militia used fire hoses. At 10:30 A.M. the Supreme Council suspended the price increase. The prime minister herself had flown to Moscow to discuss with Gorbachev the increased military activities of the Soviet troops in

Lithuania. Later she reported that Gorbachev's parting words had been "Go back and take care of the situation and restore order so that I do not have to do it myself."[17]

Upon returning to Vilnius and learning that the parliament had suspended the price increase, Kazmiera Prunskiene resigned with all her cabinet. In the same evening, *Vremia*, the official new program from Moscow, announced that "it appears that the Supreme Council is no longer in control of the situation."[18]

The next day, the *Yedinstvo* organized another demonstration assisted by Soviet troops, who set up a public address system. The demonstrators demanded the resignation of the cabinet that had already resigned. This time the *Yedinstvo* demonstration abutted a much larger Lithuanian counter demonstration, the two groups being separated by a "thin line of unarmed Lithuanian militiamen."[19]

On Thursday, January 10, Gorbachev made an appeal to the Lithuanian Supreme Council that sounded very much like an ultimatum, demanding that all acts enforcing Lithuanian independence be revoked. That evening, a large crowd of Lithuanians gathered in front of the parliament building to keep an all-night vigil.

The anonymous Salvation Committee appeared on Friday, January 11, making the claim that it had assumed all power in Lithuania. In the morning the Red Army easily occupied the Lithuanian Press Center, but as the day progressed, thousands of Lithuanians from all over the country started to arrive in Vilnius to help guard the parliament, the radio and TV studios, the television tower, and the telephone exchange. Large demonstrations against the Soviet actions in Vilnius were held in Estonia and Latvia. But in Moscow and Leningrad, too, people rallied in support of Lithuania. Gorbachev promised to use no force.

The showdown came shortly after midnight on January 13, the "bloody Sunday," when the Red Army occupied the television tower. Soviet paratroopers and armor units won a military victory while suffering a public relations debacle. Tanks rolled over unarmed civilians and soldiers opened fire at unarmed civilians. When the clash ended, the Red Army had occupied the television tower and silenced the Lithuanian state TV. But the Soviet troops had killed 13 and injured 165 civilians. Some of the injured ones died soon. All this was witnessed and recorded by Western and Lithuanian print and photo journalists and by amateurs with cameras. When a delegation from Moscow arrived in the afternoon, its members were shown videotapes of the carnage that had taken place before dawn. A particularly horrifying photograph showed a person being crushed under the tracks of a Red Army armored vehicle. The bloody mass turned out to be a woman.

At daybreak, some 200,000 Lithuanians on the Freedom Square in front of the parliament building were tensely awaiting a Soviet assault on the Supreme Council. It never came. Later on military sound trucks started to cruise along the streets of Vilnius, announcing that the Salvation Committee had imposed a curfew. Nobody paid any attention to this, neither the local population nor the delegation from Moscow that had arrived to defuse the situation.

For Lithuania, the worst was over. In a radio address, Boris Yeltsin expressed strong support for the Lithuanian leadership and appealed to the officers and men from the Russian Republic—he never used the word *Soviet*—not to participate in any anti-constitutional activity against the elected Baltic governments. The next day, January 14, in a TV broadcast from Moscow, Gorbachev and the Soviet Defense Minister, Dimitri Yazov, claimed that they had not authorized the use of force in Vilnius and that the decision to draw weapons and deploy tanks had been made unilaterally by the commander of Vilnius garrison. (That person, not named by Gorbachev and Yazov, was Major General Vladimir Uskhopchik.)[20] The victims of the attack on the television tower were laid out in the Sports Palace while the Pskov division of the Red Army left Vilnius for Latvia. Isolated acts of military depredation continued for some time. On January 23, Soviet troops seized a warehouse that stored most of the newsprint in Lithuania.

The showdown in the Latvian capital started on January 15, but in Riga the Black Berets rather than army troops carried out most of the military operations.[21] CNN reported that the Red Army troops, after listening to Yeltsin's radio address, had declined to storm Riga despite orders by the commander of the Baltic Military District, General Kuzmin. CNN took this report from Radio Riga. To the best of my knowledge, this information has never been verified. It is true that a few individual Soviet officers did condemn in public meetings the use of force against the Baltic peoples and their governments.

A few days before the shooting began, parts of Riga assumed the aspects of a besieged fortress because of the barricades being erected in front of the parliament building, the council of ministers building, the editorial offices of the newspaper *Diena* and the adjoining Radio Riga studios, the main telephone exchange, and the TV studios and transmitter, located on an island in the river Daugava that bisects the city. For barricade construction people used blocks of concrete, welded I-beams, junk, sand, and stones. Some of the barricades guarded entrances to buildings, and others stretched across the narrow streets of Old Riga, barring all vehicular traffic. Only pedestrians could crawl over or squeeze through narrow openings. To gain access to the parliament building, one had to negotiate a narrow, sharply twisting passage through a thick wall of concrete blocks, not unlike the entrance to an Egyptian tomb. These structures did not turn out to be very short-lived impediments. Some of them were removed nine months later after the August putsch, others sometime in 1992.

On Tuesday, January 15, the Interfront called a mass meeting and announced that the People's Salvation Committee had taken over the executive power in Latvia. The Committee requested that the Soviet government declare emergency conditions—"president's rule"—in Latvia and demanded that the Council of Ministers and the entire Supreme Council resign forthwith. Estimates of the size of the meeting range from 4000 to 20,000. The meeting ended with a solemn procession to the statue of Lenin in front of the Council of Ministers building. Eyewitnesses reported that the procession soon broke up and faded away.

At the same time, Anatolijs Gorbunovs, the chairman of the Supreme Council, appealed over the radio for calm and cautioned the public against provoking the Interfront with hostile acts. The Supreme Council, perhaps courting the popularity of the moment, softened recent price increases by removing income tax from the lower salaries. The complexion of the situation changed considerably in the evening, when some 100,000 people, many of them farmers from rural districts, arrived in Riga with heavy trucks and tractors to help protect the elected Latvian government.

At 4 o'clock in the morning, the Black Berets had occupied the police academy and confiscated all weapons. In the evening, they patrolled the main streets leading to the bridges across the Daugava and sporadically fired at passing trucks, presumably to discourage the use of stalled trucks for blocking the bridges that the Soviet armor units needed to cross to reach the center of Riga. One of their bullets killed a driver for the Latvian Transportation Ministry. He was the first fatality during the January days in Riga.

For many individuals the next seven days passed in tense exhilaration. During the day they went to work, and at night they manned the barricades or blocked the thoroughfares with tractors and trucks.

For the first time in most of their lives, men and women experienced the heady feeling that the future lay in their own hands.

The weather stayed cold. People built fires between the concrete blocks, sometimes sang and sometimes danced to keep warm. Musicians gave concerts all night long. Those who were not on the barricades supplied meals for those who were. Movie houses in the center of Riga remained open all night to provide warmth rather than entertainment. They charged no admission.

The blow fell on January 20 at the totally unbarricaded Latvian Ministry of Interior building across the street from the Ridzene, the most modern hotel in Riga, which served exclusively foreigners and VIP's. The Black Berets arrived at about 9:00 p.m. The prime minister, Ivars Godmanis, had issued an order to the Interior Ministry employees not to use weapons against any Soviet military formation. Nobody knows who let loose the first shot, but indiscriminate firing commenced immediately and ranged, intermittently, for some ninety minutes. When the firing ended, the Black Berets had occupied the Ministry of Interior building, suffering no casualties themselves. Outside on the street, four people had been killed and nine wounded.

The Black Berets followed the rule of shooting men with cameras first. One of their targets was Andris Slapins, an internationally acclaimed director of anthropological films whose work had taken him all over the world, including Alaska. In the late 1980s, both the Smithsonian Institution and the American Museum of Natural History had shown his films. Now he lay dead, and his badly wounded cameraman died a few days later. Wounded were also a Finnish and a Russian TV reporter. Stray bullets had damaged the lobby of the Hotel Ridzene. A few picturesque bullet holes through thick glass panels have been preserved to remind the guests, most of them foreigners, that on the night of January 20, 1991, the elite troops of the Soviet Interior Ministry did not discriminate between civilian and military targets.

The occupation of the Interior Ministry's building was witnessed by Western, Latvian, and Russian journalists. Their newspaper reports, video footages, and still photographs created an uproar in Moscow and Leningrad. As before regarding the military action in Vilnius, the Kremlin authorities denied that they had authorized the use of weapons in Riga. However, the Soviet Interior Minister, Boris Pugo, a former KGB chief in Latvia, never made an unequivocal statement that the Black Berets had acted entirely on their own. On

January 22, Gorbachev invited Anatolijs Gorbunovs, chairman of the Latvian Supreme Council, to Moscow and in a two-and-half-hour conference promised to stabilize the situation. Alfreds Rubiks, first secretary of the Latvian Communist party and the co-chairman of the People's Salvation Committee, had also been present part of the time.

Back in Riga, the Black Berets stayed on their base. On January 29, Mr. Rubiks announced that the Salvation Committee had discontinued its work and did not claim executive power. Ostensibly the three Baltic Republics returned to the *status quo ante bellum*, but the successful confrontation of the Soviet power had boosted enormously the national self-confidence of Lithuanians and Latvians as well as that of Estonians. People talked with pride about their sudden loss of fear. What they had dared to do was the stuff of nationalistic legends.

On February 7, 1991, not quite a month after the bloody Sunday in Vilnius, the Lithuanian government put to a national plebiscite the question of whether Lithuania should be a sovereign and democratic republic, completely independent of the USSR. Out of the 2.6 million eligible voters, 2.2 million, or 84.6 percent, participated and over nine-tenths (90.5 percent) cast their ballots for complete independence. The outcome of the plebescite fully vindicated the Lithuanian Supreme Council's declaration of March 11, 1990 that had precipitated the harsh measures taken by the Soviet authorities.

The Latvian government was wary of plebescites on the question of independence. Ethnic Lithuanians made up almost 80 percent of Lithuania's population, whereas in Latvia the indigenous population barely outnumbered the minorities. The official demographic figures showed 52 percent Latvians versus 42 percent Russians, Byelorussians, and Ukrainians. Poles, Lithuanians, Jews, Gypsies, Tatars, Germans, and Estonians made up the other 6 percent. The Russian-speaking population dominated urban areas. Every city showed fewer than 50 percent ethnic Latvian residents, Riga had 36.5 percent, and Daugavpils, the second largest city, had only 13 percent. Initially the Daugavpils City Soviet had rejected the Latvian Supreme Council's declaration of sovereignty and declared it inoperative within the City's jurisdiction.

Despite victories by the largely Latvian Popular Front in the last elections, it was widely assumed that the Russian-speaking population would not vote for independence from the USSR. Gorbachev, too, shared this view and made repeated suggestions that the sovereignty issue be put to a popular vote.

All through 1990, the Latvian noncommunist and pro-independence press saw those politicians who hinted at a plebescite as teetering on the brink of treason or as being incredibly naive. The January days lifted national confidence decisively, in part because Russian-speaking individuals, too, had manned the barricades, and two of them, both members of the Latvian militia, had lost their lives on the bloody pavement in front of the Interior Ministry building. On March 3, 1991, a referendum on independence, emphatically declared as consultative and non-binding, did take place. The Communist party and the Interfront urged boycott; nonetheless, 87.6 percent of the eligible voters participated and 73.7 percent of them voted for a democratic and independent Latvian Republic outside the Soviet Union. The majority of voters in every city, even Daugavpils, voted for independence. In Riga, the turnout was 84.4 percent, with 60.7 percent voting yes for independence, 37.4 percent voting no, and 1.9 percent of the ballots being declared invalid.[22] Clearly a considerable number of the Russian-speaking voters had opted for separation from the USSR.

VI

The results of the referendum strengthened the hand of the Latvian government, and it proceeded vigorously with the transition to full independence and a market economy.[23] The Council of Ministers and members of the Supreme Council immersed themselves into frenzied law, decree, and regulations making, paying little heed to their implementation. Some of the legislators viewed the passing of a piece of legislation and its implementation as one and the same thing. Too bad if the executive branch failed to enforce the law of the land; that did not concern the Supreme Council. Others felt that the new laws and decrees would become fully operational only after independence; at the moment they served the primary purpose of defining the state-to-be.

The text of the new laws and decrees, released both in Latvian and Russian languages, grated and enraged the authorities in the Kremlin and their loyalists in Latvia. Every week, the official supplement to *Diena* ("The Newspaper of the Latvian Republic") printed dozens of repealed laws and decrees that had once been passed by the Central Committee of the Latvian Communist party and the Council of Ministers of the Latvian Soviet Socialistic Republic. Laws and decrees regulating the socialistic competition between enterprises, the campaigns against social parasites, and the observance of Soviet traditions, holidays, and rituals fell by the wayside. The new legislation reinstituted Mother's Day and made Good Friday and Easter Sunday official holidays. The Soviet-type *militia* was to be converted into a Western-type, Latvian-speaking *police* by July 1, 1992. Secondary school graduates had to pass an examination in the Latvian language, and universities started to award the bachelor's degree—such blatantly Western academic degrees did not exist in the USSR. The Ministry of External Affairs issued diplomatic passports and wrote regulations about consular service abroad, totally ignoring the Soviet State Security Committee, the KGB. The new Department of Migration (i.e., the Immigration and Naturalization Service) made preparations to terminate the free movement of people between Latvia and the other Soviet Republics.

The new Customs Department, complete with border guards, attempted to regulate the flow of goods across borders. (The OMON troops systematically beat up the border guards and confiscated their weapons.) Sometime old thinking crept into the new legislation (e.g., when the Supreme Council decreed by name who would be elected to the position of the people's judge). As before under socialism, the possessive form of the noun *people* permeated the wording of the new laws and decrees.

The government assigned the highest priority to privatizing the economy. The Supreme Council created within the Council of Ministers the Department for the Conversion of State Property, whose director had cabinet status. The new Department struggled mainly with theoretical concepts. Outside the agricultural sector, very few state enterprises were privatized. The economy showed little change except for the slowly but continuously sinking output and standard of living.

The Soviet society had been so conditioned that every policy proposal, analysis, scientific paper, and editorial had to be supported and validated by appropriate quotations from Marx and Engels, plus a larger number of quotations from the supreme Soviet authorities. During the first decade of the Soviet State, the undisputed authority was Lenin; then, in the 1930s, Lenin and Stalin. In the 1940s and the early 1950s the order of precedence reversed, putting Stalin first followed by Lenin. Georgi Arbatov, the long-time director of the U.S. and Canada Institute of the Soviet Academy of Science, wrote that during his student days in the late 1940s, one was supposed to quote Stalin two or three times more than Lenin, and more than five or six times more than Marx and Engels.[24] Finally, in the post-Stalin era, Lenin alone became the supreme Soviet authority again.

By 1991, the value of the communist classics had depreciated along with the ruble, and the phrase *market economy* started to appear almost as often as the former quotations and for the same reason. Bureaucrats, politicians, and writers of editorials appealed to the alleged rules and dictates of the market economy when justifying or attacking policy proposals. The custom still dictated that neither logic nor empirical research could stand in lieu of the writ by an authority, and the new catchword, the *market economy*, filled the unaccustomed void. The market economy was also held up as the promise for the future.

In reality, market forces regulated only limited enclaves of the economy (e.g., farmers' markets, commission stores, and the wide border zone between legal and illegal commercial activities, where goods and services went to the highest bidder, provided he or she had the proper connection with suppliers). To those who knew the right people and had the money—in that order—virtually everything was available.

Essentially the three Baltic Republics had Soviet-type economies without a central plan. Inertia and personal contacts among enterprise directors, built up under the old system, kept production going, but with no central plan and no free market for finished industrial goods and raw materials, the distribution system had broken down. The government managed the economy primarily by directives. The central plan was gone, but the government assiduously planned prices, minimum consumption levels, and subsidies. For enterprises, filling government orders carried considerable advantages in the form of tax relief, easy credit, and guaranteed supplies of energy and raw materials. (The guarantee held less and less often.) As before, virtually everybody worked for the government, and the cornerstone of external economic relations was trade with the other Soviet Republics.

Nevertheless, the country unmistakably steered away from socialism. Legislative programs fostered private enterprise through the privatization of government property. New laws authorized and facilitated foreign investment and laid the foundations for joint stock companies, stock exchanges, a Western-type tax system that did not depend primarily on the old turnover tax, and a national currency. The government promised the liberation of prices by late 1992. It certainly appeared on the surface that no limitations or lack of freedom encumbered the authority of the government and the legislature.

By the early summer of 1991, a visitor had great difficulties in distinguishing pretense from reality. Officials of the Latvian government acted as if they led and administered a sovereign state, yet they kept flying to Moscow to secure various authorizations and agreements. The Latvian national flag adorned every government building, but there were plenty of red flags, too, and the omnipresent Soviet soldiery suggested occupation rather than sovereignty.

In the Russified Riga, the language of politics was supposed to be Latvian, the language of business Russian, but the line of demarcation made bends and loops and sometime vanished. Many individuals spoke both languages but for various reasons declined using one or the other, drawing up battle lines along language and culture. In the Supreme Council, most members of the minority group called *Līdztiesība* (Equal Rights) addressed the parliament only in Russian. All members of the majority, the Popular Front, were bilingual, and many of them did not hesitate to answer questions from the opposition in Russian. Those members of the Supreme Council who did not understand Latvian could listen to simultaneous voice translations in Russian, and every document was prepared in both languages. The upper echelon of the executive branch carried on its business only in Latvian, but one rarely met a militiaman on the street who could speak a language other than Russian.

The anticommunist press railed against the Soviet occupation of Latvia and every day disclosed new abuses and barbarities heretofore concealed by the Communist party. The pro-communist press saw the earmarks of fascism everywhere. An ostensibly clandestine pro-Soviet radio station, allegedly afraid of Latvian fascists, broadcasted lengthy criticisms of everyday economic and political life under the leadership of the Popular Front politicians: The worst kind of corrupting influence, for which no excuse or justification existed, was the profit motive. The Godmanis government, instead of combating this malodorous practice, joined the profiteers in their antisocial activities. The elitist government worshiped money and disregarded workers and peasants. From Moscow, the KGB chief Vladimir Kryuchkov asserted in an angry speech that all economic woes in the USSR had been caused by foreign enemies. Numerous CIA agents, masquerading as businesspeople and consultants, were sabotaging the Soviet economy.

The Soviet authorities had not entirely absented themselves from everyday life. Occasionally unknown persons shadowed a foreigner, but not very skillfully or persistently. A few Westerners were denied entry into the USSR, and a few Soviet citizens sought in vain for documents that authorized foreign travel. Telephone conversations were listened to, and the electronic eavesdropping devices in hotels kept on whirring day and night. Latvian government officials swore that the KGB disinformation mills had increased their output, but nobody could tell whether the incessant rumors about an impending putsch should be classified as deliberately planted disinformation or as pure speculations about the future. The Soviet security organs seemed to be lacking a sense of purpose and continued their activities motivated largely by habit rather than a clear mission. However, on July 31, seven Lithuanian border guards were killed at the Medininkai border post. Suspicions fell on the Riga OMON detachment.

In July, the Soviet Union went on summer vacation. In Latvia, members of the Cabinet and the Supreme Council returned home or went abroad for up to six weeks, and only skeletal staffs kept the various ministries nominally in operation. The public found it impossible to contact government officials because their secretaries had disappeared and nobody answered telephones. The universities had not yet developed the summer school habit, and the research libraries saw no reason to stay open. Industrial enterprises and nonessential retail establishments also closed for vacation, and one saw very few Soviet military officers going to their offices in the morning. Farmers, on the other hand, experienced an influx of relatives and friends, plus rent-paying summer guests, who gladly volunteered for farm work in exchange for a certain amount of produce.

After surveying the half-empty government offices and the slow tempo of the official and military life in the larger cities, I concluded that the optimum time for a coup d'état in the USSR was the month of July. But as events showed soon enough, even the putschists were reluctant to sacrifice their vacations. The putsch came during the second half of August.

NOTES

1. Robert G. Kaiser, *Why Gorbachev Happened.* New York: Simon & Schuster, 1992, p. 128.

2. Ibid., p. 131.

3. Arnolds Spekke, *History of Latvia*. Stockholm: M. Goppers, 1957, pp. 387–388.

4. Anatol Lieven, *The Baltic Revolution*. New Haven and London: Yale University Press, 1993, p. 222.

5. Abel Aganbegyan, *Inside Perestroika: The Future of the Soviet Economy*. New York: Harper & Row, 1989, pp. 30–31.

6. Ibid., p. 203.

7. Ibid., p. 227.

8. Latvian newspaper *Laiks* (Time), New York, August 2, 1989.

9. Lieven, p. 222.

10. *Laiks*, August 16, 1989.

11. *The New York Times*, March 27, 1989.

12. Michael Mandelbaum, "Coup De Grace: The End of the Soviet Union," *Foreign Affairs*, Vol. 71 (1992), No. 1, p. 168.

13. *The New York Times*, February 7, 1990.

14. *The Economist*, August 28–September 3, 1993.

15. Martha Brill Olcott, "The Lithuanian Crisis," *Foreign Affairs*, Vol. 69, No. 3 (Summer 1990), p. 43.

16. *Laiks*, January 26, 1991.

17. Alfred Erich Senn, "The Crisis in Lithuania, January 1991: A Visitor's Account." *Newsletter*, Association for the Advancement of Baltic Studies, XV, No. 1 (March 1991), p. 4.

18. Ibid.

19. Ibid., p. 5.

20. Ibid., p. 9.

21. My main sources for the events in Riga are *Diena* (The Day), "The Newspaper of the Latvian Republic" in Riga; Latvian newspaper *Laiks* in New York, as well as *The New York Times* and *The Wall Street Journal*. Another source was personal interviews with members of the Latvian Supreme Council.

22. Latvian Supreme Council Press Center, March 4, 1991.

23. The sources for this section are primarily my own experiences. I participated in some of the activities of the Supreme Council, read the official documents, and wrote a number of studies for the Economics Committee of the Latvian Supreme Council.

24. Georgi Arbatov, *The System: An Insider's Life in Soviet Politics.* New York: Random House, 1992, p. 41.

5

The Putsch

[It is] also important to note that coups can fail.

—President George Bush,
August 19, 1991

I

During the third week of August, a high-pressure system moved slowly from west to northeast above the Baltic Sea. On Monday, August 19, the Baltic region enjoyed sunny weather, but clouds started to move in toward evening. The next day began with a torrential downpour, sufficient to stop a war. The rain ended before noon, but the sky remained overcast. It drizzled all day in Moscow. On August 21, the early morning clouds dissipated and the weather remained warm and sunny for the rest of the week. This was a typical late-summer weather pattern for Northwestern Europe, but some people saw a supernatural significance in the heavy rain on Tuesday morning. Nature, they said, was weeping for the Baltic Republics. With equal justification one could claim that nature was weeping for the Soviet Union, which began to disintegrate in front of friend and foe. Perhaps the rain was merely cleansing the earth.

II

The August putsch of 1991 marks one of the great turning points in history. In seventy-two hours, the USSR, the superpower, became a collection of disunited, more or less independent states whose governments hastened to outlaw the Communist party and abolish or severely limit the power of the KGB. And yet, the seventy-two hours that changed the world did not change the daily routine of most people in the USSR. Factories and offices did not close, stores and restaurants conducted business as usual, and theaters, movie houses, and concert halls made a point of not canceling performances. Only some newspapers disappeared for a while, and most radio and TV stations went silent for a day or two.

The most dramatic events took place in Moscow, where the unrestricted presence of the Western media made this the best-covered coup d'état in history. The world saw Mr. Yeltsin climbing on an armored vehicle to defy and denounce as illegal The State Committee for the State of Emergency. Ordinary Russians thronged around the Russian parliament building, ready to defend it with their bodies, if necessary. Some soldiers, with flowers in their gun barrels, vowed not to fire on the people, but other soldiers, nervous and frightened by the defiant crowd around them, killed three civilians. The possibility of directed or accidental carnage was always nearby.

The events in Moscow took the following course. Mikhail Gorbachev, on vacation since the beginning of August, had been placed under house arrest on Sunday, August 18, at his *dacha* in the Crimea, some thousand miles from Moscow. On Monday, August 19, at about 6 a.m., the Soviet news agency TASS released a decree by the USSR Vice President Gennady Yanayev. "Owing to the conditions of his health, Mikhail Gorbachev is no longer capable of carrying on the duties of the president of the USSR. In accordance with Article 127, Clause 7 of the USSR Constitution, Vice President Gennady Yanayev has assumed the duties of president of the USSR."[1]

The decree made reference to deep and multifaceted crisis, political confrontations, ethnic tensions, chaos, and anarchy, which threatened the life and security of all Soviet citizens and the territorial integrity and sovereignty of "our fatherland." A state of emergency had been declared by The State Committee for the State of Emergency. The decrees issued by the Committee were binding to all branches of government, all officials, and all citizens of the USSR.

The membership of the eight-man Committee included some of the most powerful officials in the USSR: Gennady Yenayev; Vladimir Kryuchkov, Chairman of the KGB; Dimitri Yazov, Marshal of the Soviet Union and Defense Minister; Valentin Pavlov, Prime Minister; and Boris Pugo, Interior Minister. Standing behind the scenes was the alleged mastermind and ideologue of the plot, Anatoly Lukyanov, Chairman of the Supreme Soviet. Collectively, these men held in their hands virtually all the power in the USSR. Simultaneously with the TASS announcement, thousands of troops and hundreds of tanks and other armored vehicles began moving into Moscow.

Boris Yeltsin, president of the Russian Republic and the only publicly elected official among the key characters in the story of the putsch, challenged the legality of the Committee and urged Russians to resist the takeover. "We [the government of the Russian Federated Soviet Socialistic Republic] are completely convinced that our fellow citizens will not allow the shameless and conscienceless putschists' breach of law to gain the upper hand. We ask all military personnel to show their civic spirit by not participating in this reactionary coup d'état." In a celebrated scene standing on top of an armored vehicle, President Yeltsin called for a general strike. Celestine Bohlen, a reporter for *The New York Times*, wrote that Mr. Yeltsin spoke with a "feisty vigor."[2]

The Committee had taken over or silenced Moscow TV and radio stations, but it failed to realize that the age of cellular telephones, electronic mail, and fax machines had dawned some years earlier. Since nobody cut the electric power supply or the overseas telephone line, journalists faxed their reports all over the world. CNN transmitted directly from Moscow, while BBC and Radio Liberty relayed transmissions from Radio Russia inside Mr. Yeltsin's headquarters to a Russian audience of tens of millions. The Committee did not know how to cope with the information age.

As the day progressed, a number of military units joined Mr. Yeltsin's side. The Committee always possessed overwhelming superiority of force, but any attack on Yeltsin's headquarters at the Russian parliament building or "White House" would require shooting fellow Russians—this time, not Lithuanians, or Georgians, or Azerbaijanis. Some troops would probably refuse, and the Committee had no stomach for a military showdown.

The next day, Tuesday, August 20, Siberian coal miners responded to their president's call by going on strike. In Moscow, when the government's official newspaper, *Izvestia*, refused to print the Russian president's full-page appeal to resist the Committee, the printers went on strike, too. More and more military units and individual soldiers joined the defenders of the Russian White House, and barricades sprung up all around the building. Despite the killing of three Yeltsin supporters by nervous Soviet troops, the military situation at the White House had improved considerably.

On Wednesday, some of the Committee members flew to the Crimea to see Gorbachev. The armored units pulled out of Moscow. After the tanks had left, the Presidium of the Supreme Soviet condemned the coup and nullified the Committee's emergency decrees. In the evening, Gorbachev returned to Moscow and resumed the presidency of the USSR. On Thursday, seven of the putsch leaders were arrested or detained and the eighth, Interior Minister Pugo, shot himself. On Saturday, August 24, 1991, Mikhail Gorbachev resigned as the head of the CPSU and called for the disbandment of the Party's Central Committee. Boris Yeltsin had banned all communist party activities in the Russian Republic the day before.

The coup began in Moscow and its fate was decided in Moscow, but the conspiracy covered the entire USSR, with particular attention paid to the Baltic Republics. A state of emergency was promulgated only in Moscow, St. Petersburg, and the Baltic Republics. Lithuania had already declared full independence, while the Estonian and Latvian parliaments had voted for a transition phase to independence. To prop up the crumbling walls of the empire, a particularly firm hand was needed in the Baltics. That hand belonged to Colonel General Feodor Kuzmin, Commander of the Baltic Military District with headquarters in Riga.

The following account of the putsch in Riga is based largely on my one-week's diary and on notes of talks with various people. I never met General Kuzmin, but my apartment was directly across the street from his headquarters.

III

Monday, August 19, 1991. My day started a little after 6 a.m. Radio Latvia broadcasted its regular morning program of peppy music interspersed with news, announcements, and commercials. The newscasters repeated pretty much of what had been said the night before. I left the apartment at about 7:25. As I switched off the radio, I heard something about certain areas of the USSR being put under martial law. Must be Armenia or Nagorno-Karabach, I assumed and thought nothing more about it. The headquarters of the Baltic Military District across the street appeared no busier than usual.

As on every morning, I crossed the lovely Communard Park on my way to the Hotel Ridzene, where I usually had my meals. The hotel belonged to the Latvian government, and its guests were mostly foreigners and government officials, a good place to pick up the latest information. No fresh news caught my ear. I breakfasted with the rector of graduate education at the Riga Technical University, Mr. Brinkmanis. We discussed the differences between American and Latvian college examinations. After breakfast, I went to my office in the Council of Ministers building and during the less than five-minute walk saw nothing unusual. The streets were busy with people going to work.

At the offices of the Economics Committee (of the Supreme Council), everybody knew. Various people had picked up different newscasts. A Russian-language station had made the first announcement of the putsch at about 7 a.m. Other stations caught on, and more and more details kept coming in over the radio all through the day. The Soviet State Television, on the other hand, filled most of the morning with an interminably long movie about circus life. The solemn music, usually signaling state funerals, which allegedly worried many Muscovites, was not broadcast over the Baltic air waves.

To recapitulate the news, Mikhail Gorbachev, President of the USSR and General Secretary of the CPSU was ousted by an eight-man Emergency Committee headed by Vice President Yanayev. The key members of the Committee, in descending order of importance, appeared to be the Defense Minister Dimitri Yazov; Chairman of the KGB Vladimir Kryuchkov; and Interior Minister Boris Pugo. All of them had been appointed to their positions by Gorbachev. Some of the Latvian officials and members of the parliament I talked to that morning knew the putschists. They described Yanayev and Yazov as heavy drinkers. "Yazov is probably drunk right now." The Interior Minister's name raised everybody's eyebrows. In the late 1980s, Boris Pugo had been First Secretary of the Latvian Communist party (i.e., the de facto ruler of Latvia). Nothing at all was said about the KGB chief. This silence reflected the image the KGB had always endeavored to cultivate: You don't know us but we know everything about you.

Ever since the beginning of *perestroika* and *glasnost*, a putsch by hardliners had been predicted. Nonetheless, its timing came as a complete surprise. During the very first hours, the unfolding events stunned Latvian government officials and members of the parliament. Perhaps they expected to be arrested immediately. But as nothing untoward happened, by about 11 a.m. members of the various branches of the government recovered their confidence and sense of responsibility. The parliament and the council of ministers met and quickly adopted a joint proclamation that the State Committee for the State of Emergency was an illegal formation that had no jurisdiction in the territory of Latvia. Martial law in Latvia could be decreed only by the Supreme Council of Latvia, but the present situation was tranquil and did not call for extraordinary measures. The Supreme Council and the Council of Ministers urged the population to maintain peace and order and not collaborate with illegal powers but engage in passive resistance. No appeal was made to the constitution or laws of the USSR because "the only lawful source of power in Latvia are the Latvian people." The proclamation was read over the radio by the Chairman of the Supreme Council, Mr. Anatolijs Gorbunovs, whose ordinarily calm voice and impeccable delivery faltered just a little.

Gorbunovs is an attractive politician: handsome, unflappable, invariably polite, invariably well dressed in a country where nobody dresses well—in short, a younger version of Gorbachev. Gorbachev was born in 1931, Gorbunovs in 1942. Both men proved to themselves to be extraordinarily successful apparatchiks (i.e., professional officials of the communist party) and their careers show considerable similarities. Both had started out as *Komsomol* (Communist Youth Organization) secretaries, and both were sent to universities in Moscow: Gorbachev to Moscow State University, Gorbunovs to the Higher Communist Party School. After graduation, both worked themselves up through the ranks of the communist party. Gorbunov's first assignments were at the city-level party organization in Riga. His career took a leap upward from the local to the republic level when Gorbachev came to power. In 1985, Anatolijs Gorbunovs became the Ideological Secretary of the Central Committee of the Latvian Communist party, and in 1988, Chairman of the Presidium of the Supreme Soviet in Latvia. At some point he joined the Popular Front and resigned from the Communist party. Easily elected to the new Supreme Council, he was chosen to be its Chairman in 1990.

The upper tier of the Soviet *nomenklatura* knew one another. In the late 1980s, Gorbunovs had served directly under Boris Pugo, who was then First Secretary of the Latvian Communist party. During a 1987 interview with the Canadian political scientist, Juris Dreifelds, Mr. Gorbunovs described his boss as a capable man with a very wide circle of interests who cared about creativity and maintained close contacts with intellectuals. Gorbunovs also knew Boris Yeltsin personally.

Their families had spent a number of holidays together, most memorably during Yeltsin's eclipse from power in 1987 and 1988.

The pro-coup message in Latvia was delivered by Mr. Alfred Rubiks, First Secretary of the Central Committee of the Latvian Communist party. In a press conference broadcasted over radio and TV, Mr. Rubiks gave a warning that "there will be no joking." Any resistance to the Emergency Committee would be rooted out by force, if necessary. Some spokesmen of the Popular Front—Mr. Rubiks singled out Dainis Īvāns, First Deputy Chairman of the Supreme Council—would have to answer for their words. The First Secretary affirmed that the coup fulfilled a dream harbored by the Latvian Communist party for over a year. For the next six months he promised an unwavering return to the constitution of the USSR and more food on the table.

Mr. Rubiks's press conference created an image of a haughty individual who was gleefully looking forward to silencing and punishing his critics. After the putsch failed, he was arrested for treason. According to his interrogators, Mr. Rubik denied that he had actively supported the putsch or had threatened any person.

I spent the morning and early afternoon at various government offices. No work was being done because secretaries, legislative assistants, consultants, assistant ministers, deputy ministers, and everybody else present never stopped talking. They talked about coups in general and this one in particular, about Gorbachev and Yeltsin, about the military, about Latvian history, about the Communist party, about the presence of foreign journalists, etc. Very likely the torrent or words blocked a number of nervous breakdowns. However, the talk never veered far from the question of whether or not all of us shall be thrown out from our offices, possibly beaten, even arrested. By and large, everybody agreed that nothing would happen during the day; in the USSR, bad things happened at night.

Until the last hours of the coup, the most pressing shortage was that of reliable information. On August 19, the radio worked all day and on TV I saw CNN news in English twice. Essentially the media broadcasted fragments of defiance, but it was impossible to piece together a comprehensive picture of what was going on in Moscow or St. Petersburg. However, no channel of information announced a victory for the hardliners or at least an example or two of substantial gains. As the day wore on, people told one another more and more often that if a putsch does not succeed in twenty-four hours, it does not succeed. Interestingly, on August 19, the preponderance of rumors did not bode well for the putsch.

The news from closer to home came in clear and ominous. A column of tanks was approaching the downtown area, and the OMON troops had started to terrorize selected organizations and government offices. They had begun near their base at the outskirts of Riga and were moving slowly forward to the center of the city, where most of their targets were located.

The first session of the Supreme Council ended at 4 p.m. undisturbed by any outside force, except for military helicopters, which had started circling government offices and the old city of Riga around noon. I wanted to attend the second session, scheduled for 6 p.m. I also wanted to stroll through the downtown district and briefly stop at my apartment. The streets seemed to hold the normal flow of pedestrians—no demonstrations, no groups huddling together. Friends told me that earlier in the day bread had been sold out in some stores. This probably constituted panic buying because bread was the only staple normally available in unlimited quantities; every other food item always sold out in the course of the day.

The headquarters of the Baltic Military District literally hummed with vehicular traffic as jeeps, trucks, and staff cars arrived and departed. About a dozen armored personnel carriers parked directly on the street seriously impeded the flow of traffic. Seven pairs of fully armed soldiers guarded each side of the cluster of buildings that occupied almost one square block. The militiamen who guarded my apartment building, primarily a hostel for out-of-town members of the Supreme Council, had changed into civilian clothing. On my way to the parliament building located in the old city, I saw more soldiers than usual; nevertheless, there were plenty of city blocks without a single uniform in sight.

Earlier in the day, the position taken by the Latvian government had crystallized. The Supreme Council condemned the putsch as illegal. Next, it sent a request to all local government units and their officials not to cooperate with the military, the KGB, or any other group representing the Emergency Committee, and to treat their instructions as illegal and nonbinding. The Popular Front, the umbrella organization for the majority in the parliament, called for a passive resistance using non-cooperation, strikes, and boycotts. "Follow all the absurd official rules that regulate work, for that will paralyze production."

At the beginning of the second session of the Supreme Council, Mr. Gorbunovs gave an account of a telephone call from Colonel General Feodor Kuzmin earlier in the day. The General announced that the Emergency Committee had vested in him the executive power in the Baltic Republics. Any armed resistance would be suppressed using all means at General Kuzmin's disposal. Recalcitrant officials would be forcibly removed. In concrete terms, that might mean arresting him (i.e., Gorbunovs). "I replied that with this there was no problem."

The deliberations resumed with, perhaps, a slightly exaggerated attention to protocol and rules of order, but tension hung over the huge hall like intoxicating humidity. People fidgeted, paced between the aisles, ran outside for cigarette breaks, and whenever possible, talked to one another. The news kept getting worse. A woman was run over by a tank. The undefended Latvian TV studios fell to a helicopter-borne assault and went off the air. The OMON demolished the Popular Front's office and beat up the staff. Clearly the forces of the junta were moving closer to the parliament building. There were fears that the radio station, too, would be occupied and Radio Latvia forced off the air, but that happened only after midnight.

An extra edition of *Diena*, "The Newspaper of the Republic of Latvia," provided a noticeable lift to the sagging spirits. It arrived at the parliament chambers for distribution free of charge at about 6:30 p.m. The news printed was stale. The Latvian government's decrees and announcements had been authored and voted upon a few hours earlier by most of the same people who were present in the chambers now. Nevertheless, everybody felt that a republic that still had a newspaper cannot be dead.

The headline read, "The X-hour has arrived for all, all of us." The editorial stated that today every person is facing the zero hour for (1) deciding in which camp he or she belonged, and (2) resistance. The editorial on the first page had a footnote:

We do not know for how long *Diena* will be able to continue its work legally. There must be only one interpretation if we do not appear for a while: we do not wish to become collaborationists, and we do not wish to lie to our readers. But for now, know that we are alive, that we are here, and that we continue working.

At the time of the putsch, the mebership of the Supreme Council of Latvia consisted of two factions plus eleven independents, for a total of 201 elected representatives or deputies. The Popular Front, committed to Latvian independence, loosely united 131 representatives, most of them ethnic Latvians. Many had belonged to the Communist party but had resigned their membership before 1991. The Popular Front conducted its business in the Latvian language.

The other faction, called Equal Rights (*Līdztiesība*), was committed to a continued and close association with the USSR. All but two of its fifty-nine members belonged to the CPSU. Some of them were ethnic Latvians, but the Equal Rights faction conducted its business in the Russian language. Most of the independents stood ideologically closer to the Popular Front than to Equal Rights.

The Equal Rights faction wanted to see Latvia remaining a Soviet republic, with the Russian language at least on equal footing with Latvian. Nevertheless, some of them, perhaps a majority, felt a distaste for the military nature of the coup. As one woman put it, the USSR was an advanced and cultured country but a military coup made it look like a third-rate Latin American dictatorship. In the past, the Party had never allowed the military to play a political role.

Usually the Popular Front and Equal Rights factions were at loggerheads, but this evening, as Riga was being occupied, they almost agreed on a common course of action. The Equal Rights faction had prepared a bill that criticized the coup and called for a strict adherence to the USSR constitution. The Popular Front would accept the criticism but could not endorse the supremacy in Latvia of the USSR constitution. The two factions did not join hands.

The pressure of time caused quick adoption of the next item. The Supreme Council called for a general strike in the event that General Kuzmin prohibited the convening of the next session on Tuesday morning. The parliament's message to the constituents had to be transmitted before the OMON forced Radio Latvia off the air. As soon as the Supreme Council had voted, the Deputy Chairman, Mr. Andrejs Krastiņš, ran—literally—to the radio station.

Next, a few members raised the matter of declaring political independence. This issue did not provoke a parliamentary debate yet. Finally, the Supreme Council discussed who should stay in the chambers overnight to maintain a continuous parliamentary presence and a capability of responding immediately to unforeseeable events. The outcome was that the approximately twenty-man Presidium kept vigil in the parliament building for the next four nights.

In other offices, too, employees were making preparations for an unsafe night. Valuable equipment—telephones, typewriters, and computers—was either taken home or locked up in the safe. (Every government office in the USSR had a safe for storing secret documents, such as telephone directories.) Volunteers agreed to stay in the offices overnight to keep out unauthorized looters. Authorized looters (i.e., the Red Army or the KGB) could do as they pleased.

The Supreme Council adjourned around 8 p.m. By that time a crowd of about 500 had gathered in front of the radio station, intending to defend it. Speakers from the Popular Front, fearing bloodshed, kept trying to dissuade people from actively resisting the OMON or the military.

I left the Dom Square, where Radio Latvia studios were located, and walked about a mile and a half to the Hotel Ridzene for dinner. On my way I passed many intoxicated people. That was not an uncommon sight in Riga, but if in other days and evenings I usually encountered drunk Russian speakers, this time inebriation had crossed the ethnic line to the Latvian side. All drunks I saw spoke loud Latvian.

In the packed dining room, apprehensive waiters served apprehensive guests. Many of the foreigners were scheduled to leave the next morning on the Scandinavian Airline flight to Copenhagen, but nobody knew for sure whether the airport would be open and whether the plane would be allowed to leave. Also, would it be possible to get to the airport past tanks and military checkpoints? A fearful Danish acquaintance asked if she could call me in case she got stuck in Riga. She did not have to call because the next morning nobody interfered with the flight.

When I left the hotel, the management had turned off all outside lights because the Red Army was occupying the Latvian Ministry of Interior across the street. Two armored cars were parked near the front entrance of the building, and three Soviet soldiers, submachine guns at the ready, were kneeling next to the wall. They looked very much like children playing war. A small crown watched the proceedings from across the street. I, too, watched the eerie scene for a while. Nothing happened, not a shot was fired.

Shooting took place in another part of Riga. A car had accidentally wandered into a street occupied by the OMON troops. Somebody shouted "Halt," but the car did not stop and the Black Berets opened fire, killing the driver and wounding the passenger. Another person was killed in a collision between a civilian car and an armored vehicle.

I got home just before midnight. The radio kept on giving detailed coverage of the occupation of Riga. Much less information came in about the developments in Moscow and St. Petersburg, and one could not predict the outcome of the putsch. I fell asleep around 1 a.m.

while Radio Latvia was still broadcasting. During the night I was awakened several times by tanks revving up their engines on the street below. Those who tried to watch the armored columns from windows and balconies above the first floor level risked getting shot at.

IV

Tuesday, August 20, 1991. When I woke up, heavy rain was coming down in sheets of white and gray. The water-logged daylight made the facade across the street barely visible. Forlorn sentries huddled in doorways. Radio Latvia was silent. On my small pocket radio I located a Swedish and a Finnish station, but that did not help because I understand neither language. Never in my life had I felt a greater need for news. The telephone was still working, but those I called preferred not to talk over the telephone.

Offices in the USSR had no central switchboards. Since there were no extensions, calls could not be transferred and each number had to be dialed directly. First, I called my office. Ordinarily I was the only person working there; however, if the government offices had been occupied during the night, a military or KGB officer might be sitting at my desk. Nobody answered, which I considered to be an encouraging sign. Next, I dialed the Economics Committee number. Again nobody answered, which I considered to be a very bad sign. Actually my call had arrived at a moment when nobody manned the telephones: It was early in the morning. The Latvian government had not been overthrown, but I found that out for sure an hour and a half later.

The rain let up a little around 9:30 and I was able to leave my apartment for breakfast at the Ridzene. For the first time since 1941, I saw a Soviet officer's patrol: The officer walks in front followed by two privates with weapons held in readiness to fire. As a boy, I thought that it looked as if the enlisted men had arrested the officer and were taking him to prison. It still looked that way. Three such patrols were strolling about the Communard Park. My colleagues at the Economics Committee said that the officers looked smug.

The dining room at the Ridzene was half-full of very morose people. Many of the foreigners had left for the airport earlier in the morning. There were some new arrivals: elderly people, totally bewildered by the notion of a putsch and by the obtrusive military presence in the city. The other guests seemed to be preoccupied with their own thoughts, disinclined to share information or rumors. The staff said nothing unless spoken to.

After breakfast, I called Scandinavian Airlines and learned that this morning's flight to Copenhagen had left without any trouble. For the next two weeks, all outgoing flights had been completely booked. The first available seat was for the flight leaving on September 3.

At midmorning, when the rain stopped, people looking up at the overcast sky saw that bedraggled Latvian flags still hung on flagpoles at almost all government office buildings. I called the Economics Committee again and this time received an answer: Everyone was there.

At the Council of Ministers building, all members of the militia security detachment carried submachine guns in addition to the customary pistols. The militiamen were young, many of them Russians, assigned to guard important buildings where an official pass was required for admittance. This morning the men were extremely tense. The military and the Communist party had always made a big fuss about these "illegal fascist formations." The OMON had been charged with disarming them, and whenever that occurred, the militiamen were badly beaten. Nothing at all had happened last night.

The staff of the Economics Committee had as much information as did anybody in Riga. Allegedly four people had been killed so far and eight more seriously wounded. Everybody agreed that it could have been a lot worse. A few wondered aloud whether a sufficient amount of blood had been spilled to attract the world's attention.

Radio Latvia had been forced off the air shortly before 5 a.m. The studios were located in the Dom Square opposite the Dom Cathedral in the old city of Riga. At 4:45 a.m., a number of armored personnel carriers had arrived at the Square and opened fire, aiming above people's heads to scare away the small crowd that still lingered in front of the studio building. Next, Soviet marines, in two waves, occupied the radio station. Inside, as the firing began, the radio commentator and newly elected deputy to the Supreme Council, Mr. Aivars Berķis, announced over the microphone that Radio Latvia was ceasing transmission and started to play the tape of the Latvian national anthem. The small night staff had assembled in the main studio and, after being selectively beaten by the second wave of the marines, were thrown out of the building. One person required hospitalization. Mission accomplished, the marines opened fire at the Dom Cathedral, built in the thirteenth century and rebuilt in the sixteenth century, and then left the Square. Later in the morning, I picked up a fragment of a bullet-shattered roof tile as a souvenir.

The next target, the central telephone exchange, had been occupied by the OMON troops at about 5:30 a.m. Telephone services in Riga were cut off from the rest of Latvia and from foreign countries. However, later in the day a telex from the United States arrived for me at the parliament's communications office. I had assumed that the telex services had been cut yesterday. Actually they were cut at 2 p.m. today, the second day of the putsch.

The streets were dotted with men in military uniforms, while sound trucks kept cruising around the city calling in Russian language for peace, order, and obedience. Some kind of armored vehicles were parked in the middle of major thoroughfares, the most visible being the tanks on the bridges over the Daugava. The military objectives appeared to be intimidation and harassment. The crews did nothing, but their armored vehicles, parked in the middle of the traffic flow, threatened and inconvenienced civilians. Armored personnel carriers also darted along the streets.[3] The drivers probably did not want to crush anything, but they did not mind scraping civilian vehicles, including city buses full of riders.

As the skies cleared somewhat, helicopters resumed buzzing government buildings, and in the early afternoon they began to drop leaflets. The message from the sky proclaimed that the existing state of emergency did not threaten the sovereignty of Latvia but rather served the cause of restoring justice as well as harmony and equality among all peoples living in the Republic. The Emergency Committee's intent was to restore stability and individual human rights. Every citizen must show restraint and exercise individual and social discipline to save Latvia and the Soviet Fatherland. The leaflets were signed by six communist organization, including the Central Committee of the Latvian Communist party and the Equal Rights parliamentary faction.

The lines in front of stores were longer today than yesterday. The State Savings Bank reported that many depositors were withdrawing money from their accounts. The Executive Committee of the City of Riga—the mayor's office—tried to assure the public that the city faced no abnormal food shortage. Bakeries had seventy to eighty-day supplies of flour on hand, and it made no sense to buy extra bread in preparation for famine. The silence of radio and TV severely limited the mayor's ability to reach the public and dissuade panic buying.

In the chambers of the Supreme Council, yesterday's nervous tension and sense of futility had diminished due to heartening developments in Moscow, St. Petersburg, and elsewhere. At least one-half of the members of the parliament were holding large portable radios to one ear, listening to the Russian-language newscasts from Radio Liberty, BBC, and Voice of America as well as the radio stations from St. Petersburg. Except for the many beards and mustaches sprinkled with gray, the people's deputies looked like American teenagers carrying boom boxes.

The putsch was foundering. Boris Yeltsin was defying the putschists from his headquarters in the Russian parliament building. He had ordered soldiers, police, and the KGB to follow his commands in the territory of Russia. In St. Petersburg, 200,000 people, led by Mayor Anatoly A. Sobchak, rallied against the Emergency Committee, and an even larger number of demonstrators jammed the streets of Kishinev, the capital of the Moldavian Republic. Siberian coal miners had gone on strike in response to Yeltsin's call. There was another bit of good news: Iraq welcomed the change in the USSR and promised to establish close ties with the new regime. This was interpreted as a sure sign that every other country condemned the putsch.

Yesterday the Supreme Council expected General Kuzmin's interdiction at any moment. Nothing had happened during the night, and the next session started at 10 a.m. with 139 members present. This time the Supreme Council debated an ultimatum to General Kuzmin: Either the army evacuated all occupied buildings by 6 a.m. tomorrow, August 21, or the Supreme Council would call the population to join the "heroic Russian people" in a general strike. The resolution passed, with the Equal Rights faction voting against it. During the course of the day, a number of resolutions were adopted that placed the blame and the responsibility for illegal and socially disruptive acts during the state of emergency on General Feodor Kuzmin personally.

The news that earlier today Estonia had declared independence from the USSR electrified the chambers. A parliamentary delegation was quickly dispatched to Tallin, the Estonian capital. There was no doubt that Latvia, too, would soon declare its independence. First Deputy Chairman of the Supreme Council, Dainis Īvāns, the object of the communist party's chief's threats yesterday, had returned from Sweden. Clearly Mr. Īvāns was a brave man, but perhaps he and his colleagues sensed victory.

Today rumors started to float around that members of the Supreme Council had either fled or been arrested and only the Council of

Ministers still carried on. Another rash of rumors alleged severe fighting in Moscow, with hundreds of victims. As I stepped outside the barricades encircling the parliament building, an elderly man asked me what could be going on in the empty chambers. I replied that ten minutes ago the Supreme Council had been in session and would resume work in another twenty minutes. The man shook his head and shuffled away. I do not know whether he was a paid and trained dispenser of disinformation or whether he thought that I was one. The evening's rash of rumors insinuated that Prime Minister, Mr. Ivars Godmanis, had surrendered his authority to the Emergency Committee.

In the afternoon, the Popular Front faction in the parliament raised the matter of the leaflets that helicopters had been scattering all over Latvia. Did the Equal Rights faction endorse this? Had they willingly signed it? Initially the faction's leader, Mr. Sergejs Dīmanis, disclaimed any knowledge of the leaflets and said that he had never seen one. In the face of persistent questioning, the Equal Rights faction requested a thirty-minute recess, and thereafter Mr. Dīmanis confirmed his faction's signature on the leaflet. The gap between the two parliamentary factions widened.

The parliament adjourned at about 6 p.m. and I went to the Ridzene for dinner. Across the street from the hotel, the Red Army was looting the Latvian Ministry of Interior. Soldiers were carrying out typewriters, furniture, and files and loading them on a military bus. A group of civilians was quietly watching the expropriation from the opposite side of the street, but four young and pretty women had walked up to the door of the bus and were making fun of the soldiers. The soldiers were decent young men, they did not shoot or threaten the women; the untidy-looking lieutenant in charge seemed to be pretending that he was not there.

No matter what the military did in the streets of Riga, a group of civilians was always quietly observing them. There appeared to be a model of the group's composition: two boys, two old ladies, plus a young man and woman, probably husband and wife. Sometimes the groups were larger, but they always contained the afore-mentioned group of soldier watchers. Many Latvians told me that they had lost fear. Perhaps what was lost was the presentiment of terror that used to support the Soviet State. People found it possible not to allow themselves to be intimidated.

This evening, the sentries surrounding the headquarters of the Baltic Military District were on a higher status of alert than yesterday. They carried their submachine guns not on a sling over their shoulders but under their arms with a finger on the trigger. I don't know whether the weapons were loaded. The passersby were mostly women; they completely ignored the sentries.

The OMON allegedly stood outside the military chain of command. Aware of the OMON's reputation as thugs and murderers, the Red Army commanders always maintained that they had no contact with the OMON because the Soviet Interior Ministry set its own mission for its own troops. As I approached my apartment building, a group of Black Berets smartly stepped out of the Baltic headquarters, snappily saluted an officer, jumped in their armored personnel carriers (APCs) and rushed off. Evidently, today the Red Army had contact with the OMON.

At night, the Red Army disarmed the security detachment at the Council of Ministers building as well as the body guards of the Prime Minister. It began with a telephone call to the Prime Minister from General Kuzmin, who requested that the Latvian security detachment surrender their "extra" or "surplus" weapons. Apparently the General meant submachine guns but not side arms. A few minutes later, two APCs had arrived at the building and soldiers dressed in marine uniforms confiscated all weapons, arrested some of the detachment's officers (including the military aide to the Prime Minister), and directed the other militiamen to leave the building.

A little while later, a delegation arrived from the Baltic Military District headquarters headed by General Dudkin, who claimed that the earlier action had not been authorized by the Baltic Military District but had been carried out on somebody's personal initiative. Having apologized for the incident to Mr. Godmanis, General Dudkin ordered all Soviet military personnel to leave the premises. The arrested members of the security detachment were released, but the confiscated weapons were not returned.

I attended a soggy late-afternoon rally organized by the Popular Front. The speakers called for unity and expressed admiration for and solidarity with Boris Yeltsin. On a more practical note, First Deputy Chairman of the Supreme Council designated four locations where the public would be able to obtain uncensored news directly from their elected deputies.

After the rally, I returned to my newsless apartment. Tank engines did not disturb my sleep this night.

V

Wednesday, August 21, 1991. The rain had gone, the military occupation had not. Radio Latvia and TV were both silent, but newscasts from clandestine and foreign radio stations indicated that the putsch was failing.

Today I saw a group of five or six officers, armed with pistols, strolling around the city and observing. By and large, the officers looked affable, and some of them even smiled, but I kept wondering what exactly they wanted to see. In front of the numerous armed forces buildings—there were between 200 and 300 in Riga—stood bunches of fidgety troops who seemed to be at a loss whether to line up in a military formation or lean against the wall and enjoy the sunshine. Most of them carried rifles instead of submachine guns. All wore heavy wool coats.

On my way to the office, I witnessed an arrest. About 100 feet ahead of me on the opposite side of the street, an army patrol consisting of a noncommissioned officer (NCO) and two privates met three draft-age civilians, and for some reason the NCO decided to detain one of them. This provoked a loud argument in the Russian language. Reason and calm did not prevail, and one of the privates grabbed one of the civilians from behind, pinning his arms against his sides, and held him in that position. By now a crowd had assembled and was voicing its opinions, some of them clearly antimilitary. Needing somebody with authority, the NCO sent the other private to fetch an officer. The private dutifully ran a few paces before realizing that his rifle slowed him down. He hurried back to the NCO, handed his the rifle, and them sprinted to the Baltic Military district headquarters, a long block and a half away. Soon an army officer approached from one direction and a militia officer from another. The army officer almost ran; the militia officer walked rather slowly. It seemed to me that the military man was very happy to see the policeman. All this time, the young private kept holding the young civilian in a tight embrace. The incident on the street ended with a procession to an unknown destination. The two officers walked in front followed by the detainee, who was accompanied by his two buddies. Behind them marched the NCO and the two privates, rifles in slings across their shoulders. About a dozen civilians trailed the official party. They walked in the opposite direction of the KGB and the Baltic Military district headquarters. Soon I lost sight of them.

The upheaval of the January days had started a tradition. Memorial stones for those killed were placed in Bastion Park, where passersby bedecked them with fresh flowers every day. Each memorial stone is made of red granite, weighs at least a ton, and is marked with the engraved name, occupation, and date of death of the victim. The first victim of the putsch had been dead only since Monday, the day before yesterday, but his memorial stone, covered with flowers, could be seen in the Bastion Park today: *Jānis Salmiņš, Chauffeur, shot August 19, 1991.*

Also since the January days, entrances to key Latvian government buildings had been barricaded. To get inside the radio building from the street, one had to enter a short tunnel formed by three huge cement blocks: one on each side with the third one on top like a roof. At the end of the first tunnel, a visitor had to turn sharply to the right and enter the second tunnel, at the end of which a door to the left led into the studios. Inside the first tunnel facing the street, two armed Soviet marines were posted, one behind the other. For the last twenty-four hours, in front of them in the Dom Square a small crowd stood, admonishing and shaming them. The interlocutors were mostly elderly women who kept asking, "What will you tell your mother when she asks what you did in Latvia?" It was impossible to say what the marines were thinking. I never heard them utter a word.

As of 6 a.m. this morning, General Kuzmin had not ordered the evacuation of all seized buildings, and therefore the general strike was on. The public's response was spotty. Some establishments had gone on strike, but the majority had not. Some workers' collectives refused to obey a noncommunist Latvian parliament, some managers threatened to fire all strikers, but confusion and lack of clear instructions explained a great deal more. The parliament and the government did not coordinate their instructions. The Supreme Council ordered a general strike, while the Council of Ministers ordered numerous exemptions, including the energy, supply, transportation and communications industries; communal organizations (e.g., hospitals); and all those which were harvesting crops or engaged in food production and distribution. Nobody had listed strike-exempt establishments. Given the absence of radio and TV, some enterprise directors claimed that they did not know about the strike. A Popular Front organizer, Dzintars Rasnačs admitted, "We have no experience with this, we have never organized a strike." In accordance with Soviet reality, many enterprises "neither worked nor striked." But perhaps the main reason for the relatively lukewarm response was the growing conviction that the putschists would not win, which made the strike seem unnecessary.

During the first session, the Supreme Council considered a change in the budget and the declaration of independence. The debate did not raise emotions. Before and after, more passion was expended on much smaller issues, but the helicopter engines grew louder and louder as pilots made more frequent passes over the parliament building and the narrow streets that led to it. The parliament recessed for two hours at 10:30 a.m. for the purpose of finalizing the text of the declaration of independence.

The parliament building is located on Jacob Street, two blocks north of Dom Square. The old city of Riga resembles a wheel, Dom Square being the hub with seven streets as its spokes. All but one of them were barricaded with massive concrete slabs that prevented vehicles from reaching Dom Square. One street was left open for tourist buses, but it, too, could be quickly denied to traffic with the concrete slabs placed in readiness on one side of the pavement.

At 10:30 in the morning, lots of people were already in Dom Square. Some were participating in the general strike, and others had come to witness history being made and, perhaps, admonish the marines guarding the entrance to the radio station. A yellow city truck with a winch, operated by an elderly man and assisted by a young boy, started to remove some of the January barricades "so that cars can get through." This very innocent-looking operation carried out by two very harmless-looking individuals turned out to be a preparation for an armored assault on Dom Square. I thought that I heard distant tank engines, but I could not locate from where. Maybe the dull roar was caused by other traffic. Around 11:30, three Red Army officers appeared, ostensibly taking in the sights around the Dom Square. All three carried cameras, but none took any pictures. It can be taken as an axiom that Russian officers do not admire medieval cathedrals on weekday mornings. I concluded that an attack was imminent.

At 12:30, when the Supreme Council resumed its session, I stayed with the large crowd in the street, listening to the parliamentary proceedings over the public address system. I made sure that I had at least two different avenues of escape. The roar of the helicopter engines reached a crescendo, almost drowning out the public address system. At about 1:00 p.m., just as the Supreme Council was getting ready to vote on independence, the OMON troops came along the recently debarricaded street, riding on top of four armored personnel carriers and shouting threats and insults. Some of them aimed at us and clicked the bolts of their unloaded weapons. The crowd, which included many old women, gave a half-jubilant, half-threatening howl and surged forward to challenge the OMON.

The brash purposefulness of the OMON detachment foundered somewhat when the APCs reached the Dom Square. The OMON ordered the crowd to disperse, but the crowd didn't. As individual soldiers attacked clusters of people with nightsticks, people scattered about, only to reassemble a few moments later. Next, the soldiers attempted to break the crowd by throwing smoke grenades, but somebody always tossed them right back. The desultory confrontation, punctuated by strong expletives, lasted for less than ten minutes, when the detachment received orders over the radio to proceed against the parliament building. Hundreds of people blocked the egress from Dom Square into Jacob street. The APCs formed a wedge that moved forward very slowly, followed on each side by soldiers on foot swinging nightsticks. The crowd parted but did not disperse. After driving for about 100 yards, the APCs encountered the first Jacob Street barricade, constructed of cast iron horses, metal junk, and concrete blocks. Attempts to push the barricade aside failed. Trying a different tactic, one of the APCs hooked its winch cable to one of the concrete blocks and pulled it out of the way, much as the old driver and the young boy had done in the morning. Inexplicably, a new order came over the radio and the assault stopped. After throwing some tear gas grenades at the crowd, the APCs backed out of Jacob Street and departed. Two civilians required medical treatment.

Suddenly I became aware of silence: The helicopters had stopped buzzing the old city. I followed a circuitous route out of the Dom Square and approached the parliament building from the opposite end of Jacob Street. Near several intersections I saw parked cars, each with an army officer sitting in the driver's seat but nobody else inside.

The other end of Jacob Street was totally deserted. I heard over a loudspeaker the Popular Front's chairman, Romualds Ražuks, urging people in Dom Square to leave and use handkerchiefs to protect themselves against tear gas. All armored vehicles, he said, were gone. I, too, left and went to the Council of Ministers building, where I learned that as soon as the OMON detachment had mounted its assault on Dom Square, the Supreme Council had declared political independence of Latvia. The record showed that out of the 132 deputies present, 111 had voted for and 13 against. Nobody abstained, but eight had failed to vote. The operative paragraph of the declaration document stated that Latvia was a sovereign, independent, and democratic republic where the sovereign power belonged to the Latvian people and that the constitution in force had been adopted on February 15, 1922 by the parliament of the (First) Latvian Republic. Subsequently a number of journalists reported that the Supreme Council, fearing an invasion of the parliament building, had rushed the declaration of independence through. The deputies whom I questioned maintained that they had been completely unaware of any impending attack on the parliament.

I went back on the streets and bought all three available newspapers sold by the reporters themselves. The declaration of independence was too new for inclusion in the afternoon editions, and the main news item was still the general strike. Nonetheless, most people had heard about the declaration of independence, and their mood appeared to be very guardedly optimistic. Armored vehicles had disappeared from bridges and street intersections, and the troops were staying indoors. It became rather clear that the putsch was breaking apart. The OMON assault on Dom Square had probably been the last gasp.

I got back to Dom Square at about 6:30 p.m. The entrance to the radio station was still being guarded by two marines, and people were still admonishing them. But this time, in front of the entrance tunnel stood a militiaman who, with good humor, attempted to deflect some of the verbal arrows aimed at the marines.

A little later I participated in a huge rally organized by the Popular Front. Dainis Īvāns reported that General Kuzmin had promised to evacuate the troops not stationed in Riga this evening and that all occupied buildings would be released very shortly. The General had requested that military convoys be assisted by civilian traffic police and that other police agencies help to ensure that nobody molested Soviet military personnel. In Moscow, Yeltsin was in complete control. The putschists had boarded two planes and fled to an unknown destination while President Gorbachev was alive, well, and returning to the capital.

In the evening, the Baltic Military District headquarters was still heavily guarded with armored vehicles parked on three sides; they crept away during the night. Radio Latvia came back on the air at 9:00 p.m., Latvian TV apparently at 6:00 p.m. (I had no TV in my apartment.) The radio and TV studios had been looted, pilfered, and damaged by the occupying troops, who had broken up furniture, scattered files, smashed windows, and used offices as lavatories.

The radio journalists started by broadcasting the available information about the events in Riga, while the mechanism for collecting and analyzing international news was being rapidly reassembled. By midnight, the journalists, mostly women, had caught up with the available news and began interviewing one another. "How do you feel about males now," queried one of them, "for those who beat up our colleagues and created the unspeakable filth in our offices were men, after all?" The listener could almost see heads nodding in censure of males. But the reply was kind. "I still like men. I detest male immaturity and irresponsibility but over the last days I have met decent men who were willing to take responsibility for themselves and others." As prominent examples she mentioned Jānis Dinēvičs, the leader of the Popular Front faction in the Supreme Council, and Prime Minister Ivars Godmanis.

I thought that the journalist had articulated an important truth: Taking responsibility is the hallmark of respectable manhood. General Kuzmin refused to accept any responsibility for his actions, and so did his tank commanders when their vehicles partially blocked civilian traffic, causing several accidents and one fatality. As it turned out, nobody accepted responsibility for the putsch either.

VI

Thursday, August 22, 1991. Telephone and telex communications with the world had been restored. The Baltic Military District headquarters looked like just another office building, and very few soldiers could be seen on the streets. In the Ridzene, everybody looked happy.

In Moscow, a great deal of explaining was going on. Two news items particularly stirred Riga. Boris Pugo, the USSR Interior Minister and former First Secretary of the Latvian Communist party, had shot himself and his wife. It was a sad commentary about the relationship between Soviet leaders and the people that the most popular thing Boris Pugo ever did was to kill himself. Those who talked about his suicide—almost everybody in Riga—hardly managed to suppress a smile, and some did not even bother to do that. The second item came from Gorbachev's press conference, where he singled out the present First Secretary of the Latvian Communist party, Alfred Rubiks, who, along with Iraq's Saddam Hussein and

Libya's Muammar Khadafi, had announced his early support for the Emergency Committee.

Today, the First Latvian Police battalion began guarding the parliament building. The men looked tough and deadly. They wore helmets and flack jackets and carried submachine guns and rocket launchers. A few machine guns, too, were in sight. The Battalion expected an OMON attack at any moment. I thought that this would not happen. The OMON tactics rested on surprise and shock, but the quickly reformed Interior Ministry in Moscow had confined the detachment to its base located in the farthest outskirts of Riga. To mount an attack on the parliament building, the Black Berets would have to drive through the entire city, achieving neither surprise nor shock.

Admittedly, the Black Berets were the sharpest soldiers I saw in Riga (they even wore polished boots). Preceded everywhere by a reputation for ruthlessness and panache, they allegedly never failed to carry out their mission. But the OMON had been employed only against unarmed civilians or against border guards, militia, and police, were under strict orders not to resist. The Black Berets had never been tested against and adversary who fought back.

The Soviet State and its predecessors were masters in the use of dread, of psychological terror. Skillful propaganda supported by a few graphic examples created the paralyzing belief that the government had at its disposal omnipotent organizations that obliterated any opposition. Resistance was useless. The tsars had their cossacks and *Okhrana* (secret police); the Soviets the *Cheka* which in time became the NKVD, then the MVD, and finally the KGB. In addition, at the very end there also appeared the OMON. Everybody to whom I talked about it averred that the Riga OMON detachment was a first-rate combat unit. Actually we shall never know because the Black Berets were never tested under fire.

The Supreme Council was passing laws about national defense and also about the punishment of those who had participated in the putsch. I argued with some deputies against the unseemly haste of the punishment laws, especially since the legislators had not slept much during the preceding three nights. I may have succeeded in postponing the laws for a day; nonetheless, the accounts would be settled. The Communist party would lose legality and all its property and some leading officials would go to jail. In Moscow, the putsch leaders had been arrested, and Gorbachev was back in the Kremlin. In Riga, hardly anybody doubted that Gorbachev, too, was finished.

Finally, the legislators, the ministers, the journalists, and the people holding a vigil in the Dom Square could go home. The putsch had ended.

VII

The cleaning up. The process of dismantling the power structures and symbols of the USSR began after the putsch. All the new and sovereign republics, including Russia, did the same things, only the schedules differed. The Baltic Republics, unequivocal about their independence, moved the fastest.

Alfred Rubiks was arrested on Friday, August 23 for his part in directly supporting the putsch. *Diena* reported that the day before, Mr. Rubiks had resigned from the Communist party. Gorbachev, he proclaimed, was a traitor and a new communist party needed to be formed.

On the same day, the Supreme Council outlawed the Latvian Communist party and confiscated all its property. The law clearly stipulated that communist party membership by itself did not constitute sufficient grounds for job discrimination or prosecution.

The legal liquidation of the KGB took a day longer. Nobody defended the secret police or debated the confiscation of its property. The extremely touchy and painful item was the KGB files, which everybody feared, listed all those persons who had worked for the KGB as informants. Nobody doubted that a number of deputies, ministers, other government officials, journalists, academics, Popular Front organizers, etc., had made the list. Some deputies professed fears of disinformation (i.e., artificial files fabricated by the KGB to compromise the innocent). With few exceptions, members of the Supreme Council took a firm stand against the immediate disclosure of the KGB list of informants. "In civilized countries," it was pointed out, "such questions are resolved by special committees."

The KGB (its full name was the Committee for State Security) was declared illegal in the territory of Latvia on August 24, 1991. A day later, some members of the Supreme Council, acting without any particular authorization, entered the former KGB headquarters and physically transferred the files to a secure room in the parliament building. In 1995, several committees still wrestled with the problem of what to do with them.

The end of August of 1991 was a bad time for certain symbols and statues. In Riga, the massive monument of Lenin was removed with considerable technical difficulties but great determination during August 24 and 25. The removal crews worked all night. In a couple of weeks, amazingly lush grass and flowers had replaced the formidable statue of Lenin.

The OMON seemed to be under nobody's control, but its spirit was broken. "I understand that we have been driven against a dead end; that we are enemies of Latvia, and that we have no place to retreat to," declared the detachment's executive officer, Sergejs Porfjonovs, "but if there will be any action of provocation against us, we shall go to the end." The Latvian media prognosticated the worst: hostage taking, bank robberies, and expropriations of warehouses and stores. Nothing like that happened, and for the most part the Black Berets stayed on their base. From time to time they talked with the old bravado, and the Prime Minister's office received telephone calls from the OMON base: "Our car has been stolen, we shall come and overthrow the government." Or, "Our commander's wife is missing, probably raped; we shall come and overthrow the government." The Council of Ministers and the Supreme Council security detachments always responded by going on the highest alert status while the media embellished a little the story of the latest OMON excess.

The Latvian government applied pressure to the Baltic Military District, to the Interior Ministry in Moscow, and to Boris Yeltsin personally to do something about the OMON. In early September, the Riga OMON detachment was transferred to Russia. Later, the Latvian criminal police with the assistance of the Russian police, arrested Sergejs Porfjonovs and returned him to Riga for trial.

The Supreme Council formed a special committee to investigate the circumstances surrounding the putsch in the territory of Latvia. Almost one year later, in July of 1992, fifteen deputies, most of them members of the Equal Rights faction, were removed from the Supreme Council for having actively supported the putsch, thus opposing the sovereignty of the Republic of Latvia.

VIII

Why did the putsch collapse so quickly and so ingloriously? In the theater, the play ends and then the curtain falls; the play does not end because the curtain falls. The putsch by itself was not a major event except that, like the stage curtain, it provided a formal chronological end point to the Soviet Communist party's rule in the former USSR.

The putsch collapsed because its leaders lacked the will and the resoluteness to use sufficient military force; they did possess the capability. By Stalinist standards, the men of the Emergency Committee were too easygoing. They had no stomach for spilling Russian blood, for this time it was the population of Moscow and St. Petersburg that supported Boris Yeltsin and challenged the legitimacy of the Emergency Committee. The events in Riga mattered little.

The debacle of the putsch raises two questions: Why did a significant number of Russians suddenly take a stand against their government that was still being supported by the Red Army and the KGB? And why did the Communist party, which in the past had never lacked ruthlessness, prove to be extraordinarily weak and indecisive? Largely because Mikhail Gorbachev, the last General Secretary, who in 1991 was not particularly liked by any group inside the USSR, had fundamentally changed Soviet society.

Gorbachev's reforms had taken a direction and scope that he himself had neither anticipated nor desired. *Glasnost* gradually made it reasonably safe for individuals to challenge the authority of every Soviet institution. The liberated media showed the government in the Kremlin, the Party, and even the ostensibly omnipresent KGB to be fumbling institutions whose leaders nervously scurried about trying to shut the doors of cabinets overfilled with skeletons. The process of making history more honest led to another, perhaps unexpected, consequence: It destroyed awe before communism and its institutions and the population thus started to lose fearfulness, the presentiment of terror that had supported the Soviet state for seventy-five years. The dreaded Soviet leaders were not, and had never been, omniscient.

While *perestroika* did not succeed in elevating the Soviet standard of living, it did create the beginnings of a spirit of enterprise and a small but growing group of entrepreneurs who, operating independently of the government, despised central planning and cherished the profit motive. The suddenly opened doors and windows to the West showed, by comparison with the Soviet life, an almost unbelievable affluence. Even Soviet Marxists started comparing the successful materialism in the West to the unsuccessful materialism in the USSR.

What had happened to the Communist party? By 1991, very few brilliant people remained in it. The best men and women had resigned earlier, leaving behind mostly second-raters. The hardliners devoted to the status quo had to be either fanatics, romantic imperialists, or not very bright. Having lost most of its talented members, the Party had become ineffectual. As Lenin once said, "Everything depends on the cadre."

The Party's vitality drained away over a long period of time. For a number of years before August of 1991, the CPSU had been fighting a bloodless but emotionally charged insiders' civil war. With some exceptions, the hardliners, the reformers, the Baltic nationalists, and the leaders of every independence movement in the USSR were members or ex-members of the Communist party. The *nomenklatura* (individuals in responsible positions, selected, appointed, nurtured, and promoted by the Party) rose against the institution that had made them and guaranteed them a reasonably good life according to the Soviet standards. It had also managed to create an absurd system that affronted the intelligence of many party members.

For the post–World War II generation, selfless service in building the roseate future under communism held a steadily diminishing appeal. The older communists had been working at it since 1917 with very limited success. Moreover, the ostensibly infallible Party *had* made mistakes. Despite a few novels and plays, nobody had been able, willing, or authorized to come to grips with Stalinism. The fabric of Soviet history had a number of holes that the party dogma proved unable to patch up.

By the 1980s, many members of the Communist party were unwilling to subordinate themselves to the Party's rules, regulations, and policies. According to Anatolijs Gorbunovs, when he was the Ideological Secretary of the Latvian Communist party in 1987, "People of today understand that individual personality must not be suppressed, instead, it must be developed in order to speed up progress."[4] But the Communist party had grown into a huge apparatus—some called it "the monster"—that hampered and even stopped progress, not necessarily by design but by institutional inertia.

Memoirs of party insiders, those who had done well under the system, invariably contain much criticism directed at many of their fellow members of the *nomenklatura*, who had proved themselves to be nothing more than order takers and sycophants. Jānis Āboltiņš, deputy chairman of the state planning committee and subsequently economics minister of the Latvian Republic, characterized the Soviet "socio-economic system" in one sentence: "Dictatorship, intimidation of subordinates, and kowtowing to superiors."[5] A higher party rank automatically eliminated any need for specialized education. By definition, any superior could teach his or her subordinates anything (e.g., "how to sweep a street or how to erect a city park")[6]

Georgi Arbatov, consultant to the Central Committee of the CPSU under Andropov and former director of the U.S. Institute of the Soviet Academy of Science, wrote in his autobiography that with rare exceptions, "the system" selected and promoted people who were not very talented but who were obedient, ambitious, and unscrupulous. Indeed, inventiveness, originality, and initiative would be wasted. The Party's responsibilities, which by the time of Brezhnev's rule included virtually every aspect of Soviet life, were carried on by tiers of committees. Every proposal had to be approved by still higher committees. In this process, individual responsibility withered away. "Not once in my memory was anyone called to account for a wrong decision."[7] At the top, only the General Secretary's decisions required nobody's approval.

As long as one followed the Party's discipline, advancement did not require hard work or competence. The Party's faithful obtained higher and higher positions on the basis of attitude instead of results. Laziness and shoddy work were not bars to advancement. The more conscientious *apparatchiks* saw themselves as being engaged in constant struggle with those unwilling to work. To quote Āboltiņš again, "My sympathies have always belonged to people who did not whine but who, despite all the absurdities of socialism, did something not only for society but also for themselves."[8] But attempting anything constructive carried the risk of the Party's censure.

By the Soviet standards, the upper level of the *nomenklatura* lived very well. A Central Committee member would have a five-to-eight-room apartment in Moscow and a cottage or villa in the country. Instead of a private car, he would probably use a chauffeur-driven limousine. The republic-level officials had to be satisfied with somewhat lower level of comfort. The six-person family of the Chairman of the Council of Ministers of the Latvian Soviet Republic in 1990 lived in a three-room apartment. However, measured against Western standards, Soviet government officials and other persons in high positions lived humble lives, and they had learned this. By the summer of 1991, many members of the Soviet *nomenklatura* had traveled extensively. Virtually every Latvian official I met had been in the West. Not many had seen the United States but most had visited West Germany, France, Great Britain, Italy, or the two Scandinavian capitals (Helsinki and Stockholm) each an hour's flight from Riga. Despite the official line, they knew full well that life in the

Soviet Union contrasted poorly with the Western affluence. I sympathized with the Director of the Latvian branch of the Soviet Central Bank, who, after a business trip to Vienna, compared his lifestyle and possessions—a very nice apartment in Riga, no car—with those of the president of the Central Bank of Austria.

The putsch represented the culmination point in a war between two groups of former and present party members. On one side stood the hardliners, whose faith in the Party could not be shaken by mere events, men and women with a boundless capacity for forgiving the Party anything. (In my talks with staunch and unabashed communists I never succeeded in discovering the reason why the Party deserved so much forgiveness.) On the other side stood the reformers and apostates, for whom the Party had become an aberration of communism and socialism, as well as a barrier to progress and a better life. In a sense the hardliners were idealists for whom faith had triumphed over reason and reality. One would be able to make a stronger case for their idealism had they been less privileged when they attempted to maintain the status quo by employing military force.

The leaders of the putsch had made impressive careers within the system, but as a consequence they had become victims of the system. Rising through the Party's committees, they never had to take full responsibility for anything. Committee members did not make decisions; they concurred with them while the origin of the decision often disappeared in the party's labyrinth. Bold and resolute decision making and dramatic initiative taking do not come naturally to basically obedient men in their fifties and sixties.

Gennady Yanayev, who replaced Gorbachev by assuming the role of acting president, had started his career as a *komsomol* official, rising to be chairman of the USSR Committee of Youth Organizations and deputy chairman of the Soviet Friendship Society. The former dealt with foreign youth movements, and the latter maintained nongovernmental contacts with foreigners. After becoming a member of the Supreme Soviet as a labor union representative, Yanayev was elected to the politburo in 1989. He was Gorbachev's choice for vice president and was narrowly elected on the second ballot. Yanayev had no previous public image of his own and had to live down the charge of being too minor a figure for the important position of vice president of the USSR.

The communist party officials knew very well that the secret police was keeping tabs on every one of them. For the excellent reason of self-preservation, the Party, in turn, monitored the KGB, never allowing it a voice in internal politics. From the very beginning of the Soviet State, the Communist party recognized the latent political power resting in the armed forces; they, too, had to be kept out of politics. As a consequence of fear felt by the members of the Central Committee, the director of the KGB and the defense minister had never been allowed any decision-making power outside their own organizations. Also, the historical men-on-horseback usually cut youthful and audacious figures. Kryuchkov and Yazov, both sixty-seven years old, were the oldest among the leaders of the putsch. Marshall Yazov probably joined the others because he was angry that the recalcitrant republics had made the drafting of soldiers in the Red Army virtually impossible.

After the putsch had foundered, members of the Emergency Committee turned to Gorbachev, the president whom they had deposed just three days earlier, for guidance, understanding, and forgiveness. The conventional Kremlin *apparatchiks* did not measure up to the defiant and decisive Boris Yeltsin or the Estonian and Latvian leaders, most of them former members of the Communist party who, in the middle of the putsch, declared full independence for their republics. Without any military backing they assumed the responsibility for an action that could have cost them their lives if the putschists had won.

At the Soviet pinnacles of power, information arrived in a filtered form. Subordinates made sure that the important men and women heard what they liked to hear. The Party's persistent lies and falsification of history had left many of its leaders actually believing in the official line. Very likely Mr. Kryuchkov did see the Soviet economy being torn apart by Western intelligence agents masquerading as consultants and businesspeople. *Perestroika*—reorganization of the economy—constituted sabotage of the State's economy, while *glasnost*—openness—meant revealing of State secrets. Both offenses called for stern punishment. The leaders of the putsch completely failed to perceive that the society had changed and moved away from unquestioning obedience to the authorities.

Throughout the putsch, the Red Army kept hesitating. The heretofore disciplined tool of the Party was undergoing a painful soul searching. The retreat from Afghanistan and the impending withdrawal of Soviet garrisons from the former satellite countries had lowered the morale of all ranks. At home, a vociferous organization, called Mothers of Soviet Soldiers, kept up a barrage of accusations that sadistic hazing of junior enlisted men in the Red Army had left their sons crippled or dead. This did not speak well of the professional standards of Soviet officers and senior noncommissioned officers. The unprecedented civilian criticism of the Red Army angered some officers and depressed others. Clearly, the Soviet armed forces, too, needed reforms.

Just a few years earlier, the Red Army had vigorously and bloodily suppressed nationalist demonstrations in Azerbaijan and Georgia. It had resolutely moved against the Lithuanians in January of 1991. But this time, in August of 1991, it faced a Russian population in Moscow and St. Petersburg; the Baltics were merely a side show. The army exercised restraint, in part because the high command did not think that the troops would obey orders to shoot, in part because the commanding officers of the various military units saw no visible public disorder to suppress. The Emergency Committee had exaggerated. Except for the troop movements themselves, nothing unusual was happening in the streets of Moscow, St. Petersburg, Riga, and elsewhere. The army came, waffled for a while, and then departed. Very likely the fear of adverse world publicity reenforced military restraint. By early 1991, many foreign journalists were reporting from inside of the Soviet Union. The outbreak of the putsch set off a veritable avalanche of journalists rushing in. The Soviet border guards had received no orders to stop them, and the new arrivals managed to catch the last day and the immediate aftermath of the putsch. (During the first week after the army's withdrawal I met American, British, Hungarian, Japanese, and Russian journalists in Riga.) The KGB personnel, perhaps sensing more clearly than anybody else that the empire had come to an end, played a very passive role.

The Emergency Committee did not include any populists; they appeared on the scene after the breakup of the USSR. The leaders of the putsch had no gift for oratory and no experience with persuading the public. In Soviet politics, persuasion of the people was carried on in small groups or on a one-to-one basis by party agitators. Let the Western politicians worry about public relations. The top Soviet leadership only commanded and announced. No need to win the public over, analyze the issues, or worry about one's image on the TV screen. Gorbachev, who did show concern about his public image, had introduced something new into Soviet politics for which the putschists had no appreciation whatsoever. Their TV appearances created an impression of impotence and fear, or possibly ill health and inebriation. Numerous Western reporters mentioned Mr. Yanayev's trembling hands. Summing it up, the Emergency Committee, never having the will, did not develop the ability to enforce its decrees, while the population no longer heeded exhortation or threats by the authorities.

NOTES

1. The texts of the official decrees and Mr. Yeltsin's countercharges were printed in the Latvian newspapers *Latvijas jaunatne* (Latvian Youth), and *Diena*, Riga, August 20, 1991.

2. *The New York Times*, August 20, 1991.

3. The U.S. Army's personnel carrier (APC) is a track vehicle; the Soviet Army's APC was a wheel vehicle.

4. "Intervija at Anatoliju Gorbunovu" (Interview with Anatolijs Gorbunovs), *Baltiešu forums* (Baltic Forum), IV, No. 2 (Autumn 1987), p. 42. The interview took place at the Chautauqua Institution in upstate New York.

5. Jānis Āboltiņš, *Biju biedrs, tagad kungs* (I Was a Comrade, Now I Am Mister). Riga: Jakubāna un Hānberga bibliotēka, 1992, p. 69.

6. Ibid., p. 42.

7. Georgi Arbatov, *The System: An Insider's Life in Soviet Politics*. New York: Times Books, 1992, pp. 223–224.

8. Āboltiņš, p. 41.

6

Groping Toward Democracy and a Free Market

The old system collapsed like a rotten shack. They [the former *nomenklatura*] threw their party membership cards in the rubbish and grabbed commanding posts in commercial structures.

> —General Alexander Lebed,
> Commander, Fourteenth Russian Army
> in Moldova, retired in 1995

We have people out there who buy cheap and sell dear. The government must do something about this.

> —A member of the Latvian
> Supreme Council, autumn of 1991

I

Instead of saving the Union, the putsch foredoomed it. The Soviet empire started to come apart in late August of 1991. To everybody's astonishment, the superstructure of a seemingly powerful state disintegrated like a dynamited building shown on a newscast. First comes a muffled explosion while the building seems to shrink in height a little. Next, the structure starts to wobble, the walls buckle out, and then everything comes crashing down. It takes a long time for the dust to settle.

What exactly collapsed? First and foremost, the Communist party as an institution that was synonymous with the Soviet state. Some, not all, upper-tier leaders of the government, the military, and the security agencies fell from power together with their party. Other former party officials of high rank filled the top government positions in all of the new, noncommunist states, if not immediately after independence, then a year or two later. For example, Geydar Aliyev, a former member of the politburo, was elected president of Azerbaijan in 1993. A year earlier in 1992, Georgians elected as their president Eduard Shevardnadze, a former foreign secretary of the USSR and member of the politburo. Between 1972 and 1985, he had been first secretary of the Georgian Communist party. Nursultan A. Nazarbayev continued as president of Kazakhstan, and his popularity never waned. The last Soviet-era presidents of Kyrgistan, Moldova, and Turkmenistan ran unopposed for reelection in 1991 or 1992. Each of them won with at least 95 percent of the popular vote, reminiscent of Soviet elections, where the single, party-selected candidate never failed to receive almost all of the vote. Leonid M. Kravchuk, a former party official and chairman of the Soviet Ukrainian parliament, became the first elected president of the independent Ukraine. In the Baltic States, a formed deputy chairman of the Estonian Council of Ministers under the Soviet rule, Edgar Savisaar, headed the first government of independent Estonia. The very popular Anatolijs Gorbunovs kept his job as chairman of the parliament of the Latvian Republic. First secretary of the Lithuanian Communist party, Algirdas M. Brazauskas, was elected chairman of the parliament and acting president of the new republic in 1992 and president in 1993. All these men had resigned from the Soviet Communist party at some point between 1989 and 1991.

No new cadre stood ready to replace the old *nomenklatura*. Consequently, most of the second- and lower-tier officials and managers survived the dramatic change of the political system. With very few exceptions, the old enterprise directors, school principals, university administrators and professors, collective farm chairmen, chief engineers, judges, military officers, and variegated bureaucrats kept their jobs. Only the numerous party workers and secretaries faced sudden unemployment.

Nowhere in the world are positions of authority and responsibility held by unknown individuals. In the old USSR, nearly all prominent and ascending persons belonged to the Communist party. The last genuine communist probably died a long time ago but, using U.S. terminology, managers, administrators, and professionals in the USSR worked in a closed shop, where party membership was a condition of employment. It could not be otherwise but that the former communists would lead the new republics away from communism. Many of them worked conscientiously at effectuating a transformation. The turnabout engendered few wrenching psychological conflicts because the Communist party had created a system both absurd and silly. It had been abundantly clear for a long time that the system did not and could not work. So it came to pass that people who just a few years earlier had been building communism and denouncing fascism and capitalism in the West became opponents of communism and builders of capitalism or a Scandinavian-type socialism.

After independence, political, constitutional, and economic issues dominated public discussion, as reflected in the record of parliamentary deliberations and the media. What did not happen was a coming to terms with the communist past: an official acknowledgment that the Communist party and the Soviet State had committed crimes against humanity and that a number of living individuals carried at least moral responsibility for evil deeds committed against the innocent. Instead, the society preferred euphemisms because too many people, freely or under compulsion, had collaborated with the KGB. Those who had been executed, deported, or imprisoned were classified as "the repressed ones." The survivors among them made up a strangely quiet group that formed clubs and talked about "the policing of the battlefield" (i.e., finding out what exactly happened to whom). Gradually the names of "the repressed ones" were being rehabilitated; many of the persons themselves had already died. In the Latvian War Museum in Riga, called the "Gunpowder tower," brightly lit display cases in dark halls contained ever-lengthening lists of thousands of names of those who had been falsely "repressed." All the relevant Soviet laws were cited. Some of the individuals who administered the rehabilitation process once had administered the arresting and deportation process. Experienced help is never out of work for long.

The embarrassing past will not go away. The question of whose collaboration with the KGB had made a victim of somebody else will trouble all former Soviet citizens until the end of their days. Every repressive regime ultimately rests on a large number of more or less willing servants, and this scatters the seeds of something like the terrorist Bader-Meinhof gang in the former West Germany. Some twenty years after the end of World War II, young men and women, children of prosperous former officials and businessmen of the Third

Reich, formed terrorist groups lashing out against the complacent society as a belated denunciation of their parent's hypocrisy and careerism.

As one of the first official acts, every government of the new and independent former Soviet Republics abolished or at least nationalized the KGB. According to an apocryphal story that circulated throughout Riga in late 1991, after Boris Yeltsin had closed down the KGB in Russia, ordinary people continued coming to the old offices of the secret police for the purpose of denouncing their neighbors. The slow death of ingrained habits makes the transformation of society and economy extraordinarily difficult.

II

The great nineteenth-century English economist and philosopher John Stuart Mill saw human beings as victims of the tyranny of antecedent circumstances. For the Soviet peoples of 1991, the antecedent circumstances had been purposefully molded for several generations by the Communist party. It never left them alone. The Party explained the world to them, monitored their behavior, inculcated and reenforced the appropriate attitudes, took care of them, rewarded them with medals and perquisites ("privileges"), and corrected and punished them. The official version of Marxism and Leninism repudiated individualism and extolled collective action under the proper leadership. The masses, the leaders firmly believed, needed much guidance by the vanguard of workers and peasants, the Communist party. The wise Soviet manager and specialist, as well as the artists and scientist, made a point of attributing a large part of his or her success to the inspirational guidance received from the Communist party.

By definition, the Party never erred, consequently, industrial failures, the few reported transportation disasters, or the infrequently acknowledged shortages were caused by saboteurs, Western intelligence agents, and other vermin. The hunt for enemies of socialism brought the KGB into every sphere of Soviet life. The adage that only those who do nothing never make mistakes had no standing in the Soviet Union, where decision making by committee saved managers from being regarded as saboteurs if something they did went wrong.

During Khrushchev's tenure as first secretary, the Party's grip on Soviet life relaxed a little, but with Brezhnev's coming to power, virtually everything became the Party's business again. The Party's ubiquity eventually turned into a political liability. In the public's view, the few improvements in Soviet life did not offset the innumerable failures and shortages. The Party got blamed for everything, including such apolitical events as traffic accidents or adverse weather conditions resulting in poor harvests.

It has been asserted that capitalism fails to satisfy the psychological needs of the less successful. In sharp contrast to the Western ethos, personal failure and the accompanying sense of guilt and inadequacy did not exist in the minds of most Soviet citizens. It was the system that caused every kind of failure. The system explained not only perverted economics and politics, but also alcoholism and domestic violence, divorce and the abandonment of children, pilferage at the workplace, and unsanitary conditions in public lavatories.

On a bright and sunny autumn afternoon in 1991, a drunk had passed out in the middle of the sidewalk near the Hotel Ridzene and the Latvian Academy of Fine Arts. A small crowd had gathered around him, and as I passed by, I too stopped to look. Next to me stood two elderly ladies who, I thought, would be particularly censorious of disgusting drunkenness. "Alas," one of them sighed, "you see how our system has ruined this man." Academician Leonid Abalkin, director of the Institute of Economics of the Russian Academy of Science, labeled as "vulgar sociology" the endeavors to create "a mass of personal conveniences, a certain comfort level," by pointing to the "determining forces of external circumstances."

After all, it is so easy (and pleasant) to ascribe one's personal disorganization, social passivity, and outright sloth to . . . socialism, totalitarianism, or Stalinist excesses (take your pick).[1]

A free market does not flourish in a setting where every shortcoming is regarded as a sign of systemic failure and no individual carries any personal responsibility for anything. The two phrases heard again and again by Western advisors in 1991 and 1992 were "You don't understand our system" and "It's the fault of our system." Nobody had been accustomed to individual responsibility and accountability.

Moreover, Soviet economic agents never had to develop the mentality for coping with uncertainty. As long as an enterprise fulfilled its plan, it need not worry about selling its product. The feeling that it was the government's responsibility to create a market outlasted the planned economy and carried over to the post-Soviet period. During the first months, nearly everybody kept waiting for instructions from above, and all the new governments took a good deal of criticism for not setting comprehensive production norms and failing to promulgate an adequate number of regulations.

The collapse of the Soviet empire created a vast area for a potentially free market. After a feeble and hesitant beginning, privatization of government enterprises started to gather momentum in 1992, and many of the new private businesses showed themselves as being capable of replacing and besting the moribund government enterprises. As the new businesspeople faced the chaotic beginning of a free market with a high probability of failure as its main characteristic, the idea of victimhood had considerable appeal. It saved face. When I returned to Riga in 1993 and 1994, the mafia and the former KGB agents had replaced the system. Conspiracies and sabotage by organized crime groups and the former KGB agents allegedly explained bank failures, corruption, bankruptcies, tax evasion, and the painfully slow economic progress. Pitted against powerful and ruthless criminal adversaries, individual businesspeople and depositors had no defenses and could not be blamed for going under. The failure of governments to bail out bankrupt businesses and the allegedly defrauded depositors opened up the charges of widespread corruption among politicians, who, thinking only of themselves, supposedly collaborated with criminals. For many people, the economy and the society needed a powerful master.

In the USSR, the government bore the primary responsibility for the ubiquitous genteel poverty, the long lines in front of stores, and the depressing communal apartments. With its inflexible commitment to central planning from Moscow, the Soviet government had brought to the brink of ruin the largest and potentially the richest country on earth. One would have thought that after living for many decades under an inept and cruelly repressive regime whose victims numbered in millions, the people would chant almost in unison, "that government is the best that governs the least." Yet people's faith in government, big government, had remained unshaken. In the majority's view, only government could solve society's economic problems. Life in the broadest sense needed regulation. People themselves could not be trusted.

Historically, Russian political beliefs have stretched between two poles: nearly complete trust in government, tsar or commissar versus total negation of any authority. Many monarchists and Stalinists found solace in repeating the plaintive theme: If only the tsar, or Comrade Stalin knew what was going on, he would right all wrongs. Alas, corrupt and self-serving officials stood between the wise and good leader and his people. After Stalin's death, the Party picked up the mantle of the benevolent and omniscient leader, but the visibly growing cynicism and careerism among its officials ultimately eroded its inherited authority.

Around the periphery of the empire, people of the Baltic, Caucasian, and Asian Republics craved for their own, independent governments, instead of the marionettes whose strings were manipulated from Moscow. But on the periphery, too, the argument for a limited government clashed with the firm conviction that human beings need comprehensive regulation to forestall societal disorder and crass inequalities in income distribution. The disposition for big government appeared to be in the genes when a group of elderly emigrés, after almost a lifetime spent in the United States, argues vehemently for the absolute necessity of having a ministry for culture, sport, and tourism.

Anarchism, the other extreme that dismisses all forms of government as oppressive and undesirable, also found resonance in Russia. The Christian anarchism of Leo Tolstoy (1828–1910) and the militant anarchism of Mikhail Bakunin (1814–1876) and Peter Kropotkin (1842–1921) attracted numerous passionate followers. Very militant groups of anarchists emerged during the 1905 revolution and the Russian Civil War. After the collapse of the USSR, many former Soviet citizens viewed the free market as a manifestation of anarchy; most of them did not like what they saw. It hurt to see a number of undeserving people doing remarkably well.

III

In early October of 1991, not quite two months after the putsch, I began teaching in English a course in the principles of economics to a class of fifty-five Latvian and Russian graduate students who wanted to enroll in an American Masters of Business Administration program that would be offered by the Riga Business School in 1992.[2] During the first lecture, I asked the students to name the greatest social value. Two or three of them managed to overcome the paralyzing fear of mispronunciation and said "equality." Many heads nodded in agreement. At that moment my students' idealism formed by a socialist education had not been beclouded by fundamental doubts. When I returned in 1993 and again in 1994, none of my almost 200 economics students mentioned equality as a social value.

Among the ideals men and women have been willing to die for, equality stands near the top, just a little below freedom. Socialists, always and everywhere, have claimed property rights over equality But the Soviet egalitarianism included "not only equality of opportunity, an accepted principle in Western democracies, but also equality of outcome."[3] It leveled incentives for personal achievement and excellence until the well-worn saying "we pretend to work and they pretend to pay us" characterized the Soviet industry. Managers did not favor that kind of egalitarianism at the workplace,[4] but the workers had been told time and time again that they were the privileged class that set society's norms in a workers' state. Material success that elevated one above one's neighbors constituted antisocial behavior, and popular egalitarianism justified any action taken against the successful.

The first successful businesses in the former USSR were private banks and various trading enterprises. Soviet citizens had been taught since their elementary school days the Marxian dogma that banking and trading exemplify unproductive labor that, in contrast to the production of goods, creates no value. Therefore, profits in banking and trade must come from "speculation," from the exploitation of the people.[5] A successful merchant or banker would most likely be (1) a mafioso, (2) a former KGB officer, or (3) a foreigner or an agent of foreigners. A large part of the public viewed them with suspicion and hostility, which frequently took the form denunciation to the authorities, pilferage, and vandalism. The feeling persisted that profit in the form of money was somehow dirty, whereas perquisites, the main form of material reward under the Soviet system, were not. Consequently, only a government appointment legitimized success. Vulgar accumulation of money by private businesspeople deserved only scorn. After the breakup of the USSR, living conditions worsened for most people. The sight of the nouveau riche businesspeople driving luxury cars and patronizing expensive night clubs did nothing to lighten society's disdain for private entrepreneurs.

All the new post-Soviet states had inherited from their past the legal and moral illegitimacy of private ownership of business. The Soviet constitution did not recognize private property rights in the means of production. The new constitutions, adopted after the fall of the USSR, reinstituted private property, but people who had grown up under the Soviet system never developed a sense of the subjective legitimacy of property rights (i.e., the conviction that property rights are natural and necessary and should be respected and enforced).[6] In the still prevailing scales of justice, the rights of tenants and employees outweigh the rights of the owners. No stigma attaches to pilfering by workers because they are ostensibly poorer than the new owners of businesses. Starting in 1992, numberless retail establishments mushroomed throughout the former Soviet Union. The sales clerks found themselves in a good position for stealing merchandise and money. Given the muddled judicial system caught between the old laws, which always championed the worker, and the emergent laws of property rights, which the public did not fully understand or accept, the employer's only recourse was to fire the thief. No court would convict him or her.

Theft in the former Soviet Union sometimes took fantastic dimensions. Trains stopped because somebody had stolen switches or rails. The employees of the signals and communications department of the Latvian State Railroad complained in an open letter to the President of Latvia that between 1992 and 1994, somebody had stolen 254.5 kilometers (165 miles) of overhead electric cable and well over a thousand switches and transformers containing copper and other nonferrous metals.[7]

In Russia, corruption and bribery are perpetual problems, no different under President Yeltsin than under the tsars and commissars before. The old Soviet system had the peculiarity that having money was not enough for obtaining goods and services. In addition to rubles, one needed authorizations commonly procured through personal connections. Today, the buying of goods and services requires nothing more than money, but one still needs connections—they can be purchased—for getting a set of licenses to open and operate a business, to export or import, or to lease office space. Very good connections are needed to rent an apartment. A bureaucratic system that fixes all problems by issuing regulations has many clerks and officials empowered to authorize or to deny authorization while earning very modest salaries themselves. A modicum of power coupled with impecuniousness nourishes bribe taking.

IV

In October of 1993, the leader of a Lithuanian criminal gang, known as the Vilnius Brigade, ordered the assassination of Vytas Lingys, an investigative reporter for the newspaper *Lietuvos rytas* (Lithuania's Morning). Lingys had written a series of stinging articles about the extortion and drug smuggling activities of the Vilnius

Brigade. A gang member gunned him down in broad daylight outside his home. This case differed from many others because the trigger man, Igor Achermov, and the gang leader, Boris Dekanidze, were caught. Currently, Igor Achermov is serving a life sentence in a Lithuanian jail. Boris Dekanidze received the death sentence, which was carried out on July 12, 1995. Seven years earlier, in 1988, he had lived in the United States reportedly serving as a body-guard to a Bronx mafioso. Lithuanian Interior Ministry announced that Dekanidze's body had been buried in an unmarked grave at a secret location. According to *The Baltic Observer*, many Lithuanians believed that the authorities had faked the execution and that Dekanidze, having bribed himself out of jail, had departed for some pleasant and safe location.[8]

On March 1, 1995, two unknown men shot to death the popular and highly respected Russian TV journalist Vladislav Listyev. The murder took place at 9:15 p.m. in the stairway of his apartment building located in the center of Moscow. Known as a vocal crusader against crime and corruption, Mr. Listyev had been appointed Director General of the Russian Public Television Ostankina channel. At the time of his death, he was reorganizing the Ostankina channel and taking measures to prevent dubious firms from buying air time. Mr. Yeltsin called the assassination "a tragedy for all Russia" and promised that swift action would be taken to apprehend his murderers.[9] Many Russians doubted his sincerity because the government had shown a persistent inability to suppress the activities of criminal gangs.

In an optimistically titled book, *How Russia Became a Market Economy*, Anders Aslund, economic advisor to the Russian government from 1991 to January of 1994, quotes the Russian Ministry of Interior estimates that in 1994, 5491 criminal gangs with about 100,000 members operated in Russia. Organized crime allegedly controlled some 40,000 Russian enterprises.[10] The accuracy of such estimates may be doubted, but everyday news makes it only too evident that organized criminals, commonly called *the mafia*, operate on a vast scale throughout the former USSR.

Businesspeople encounter extortion regularly. The mafia demands protection money, and the penalty for noncompliance ranges from goons pouring gasoline on meat, to mysterious explosions, to kidnaping and murder. This has generated demand for firms selling security services. Sometimes the sellers are the extortionists themselves. The most common allegation heard is that behind every large-scale criminal activity looms the former KGB. Some argue that the KGB had organized the web of extortions; others—sometimes the same people—aver that former KGB agents provide the best protection against the lawless mafia. The probability that the mafia could organize massive theft and smuggling-out of Russian nuclear materials has been of great concern to the West.

Along the new frontiers, a large portion of the customs duties remains uncollected due to the corruption and poor training of the customs officers and the adroitness and organization of smugglers. For example, a small portion of the Russian Federation, the Kaliningrad region, is separated from the rest of Russia by Lithuania and Belarus. Shipments of oil from Russia to Kaliningrad cross Belarus and Lithuania duty-free. Somehow the oil winds up in Estonia, Finland, Latvia, and other countries. The allegedly mafia-run oil distribution channel obtained Russian oil at the subsidized price of 38 cents a gallon and sold it for $1.16 to $1.29 a gallon in 1994.[11] No tax was paid to any government.

The mafia does not fear visibility. Mercedes and BMW limousines serve as symbols of office for the Russian equivalent of the mafia dons. Their soldiers love black leather jackets. Something like a uniform helps to intimidate the objects of the extortion racket. Crude tattoos on hands and arms, more rarely on faces, mark the lowest ranks of criminals, the *urki* (thieves), whom the mafia employs strictly on a temporary basis. In every larger city, leather-jacketed young men hang around certain restaurants and nightclubs or loll in the limousines parked outside. Inside, somewhat older men in expensive imported suits socialize within a shouting distance from their bodyguards. Turf battles among the various mafia groups explain a large part of the rising homicide rate.

For a long time to come, the post-Soviet society will continue carrying the earmarks of the Soviet Union. The old USSR always was a lawless state. The authorities demonstrated a paranoic concern for internal security but very little regard for law. The legal system and the Soviet constitution did not limit the power of the Communist party. Many persons had a party rank or connections that placed them above the law. It was always a more serious crime to murder a communist party member than an ordinary person. The notion of a contract as a morally and legally binding obligation died during the early years of the Soviet state. In the post-Soviet states of the early 1990s, the term contract appeared to be nothing more than another import from the West, meaning "an agreement that can be altered or ignored unilaterally."

The burgeoning criminal activities require an army of career criminals. The recruitment presented no difficulties. The old Soviet media covered crime cursorily and ambivalently. Crime, ostensibly a pathology plaguing the capitalist society, had no theoretical existence in the USSR. The realities of life, however, demanded some reporting of crime and punishment. The numbers involved turned out to be considerable. The law reserved the harshest punishment for political offenses. In contrast to the enemies of the Soviet state, criminals were "socially friendly."[12] Every memoir of the Soviet labor camps dwells on the cruel conflict between the political prisoners and the convicted criminals, who served as the trustees. [13] Near the end of the Soviet Union, many of them were amnestied together with the political prisoners.

After the putsch, the ranks of career criminals have been swelled by entrants who had been accustomed to a high life under the Soviet regime but were facing unemployment now: ex-military and KGB personnel, and the second-rank professional athletes.[14] Criminal life also appealed to a number of young people, who saw few good prospects in legal employment and much wealth in organized crime. In the Caucasus region, many of the paramilitary groups warring there allegedly maintain links with organized crime, including occasional exchanges of personnel.

The army of criminals enlisted under the banner of various mafia groups confronts a law enforcement system with few lawyers—an almost unnecessary occupation in the USSR—and very many underpaid and underorganized policemen. The courts and laws that they serve have never dealt with extortion and property crime. Only one thing never changes: Many criminal offenses are committed under the influence of alcohol. Other drugs appear to be far less popular.

All presidents of the new post-Soviet Republics have placed the highest priority on developing a well-ordered legal system that, among other benefits, would help to attract foreign investment. Unfortunately, the creation of laws requires time. In the Baltic Republics, numerous laws were written between 1990 and 1992 as the former Soviet Republics hastened to distance themselves from the Soviet legal system. Due to internal inconsistencies and contradictions among them, many of these laws had to be rewritten. It will take a number of years before the new legal systems become truly well ordered. It is difficult to predict how long will it take for the new governments to develop the willingness to enforce the already existing laws. The web of connections protects even those officials and other important persons who should be serving time in jail.

V

Every former Soviet republic started its career as an independent state saddled with the inheritance of the Soviet-type economy without a central plan. In 1991, the production system floundered badly because the distribution system had broken down.

The Soviet leaders, and perhaps the Russian people as well, were enamored with large size. The largest country in the world had large industrial plants equipped with large machines. Large dams regulated the flow of large rivers, and large agricultural tractors lumbered over large state and collective farms. The philosophy was centralize, consolidate, and exploit economies of scale! In cities, a few centralized generating plants transmitted steam heat and hot water to all buildings via an extensive system of piping that lost as much as 50 percent of the energy through leaks and radiation into the air due to deteriorating insulation. Large plants located in one of the Soviet republics frequently produced for the entire Union. The Lithuanian factory *Banga* made all TV tuners in the USSR, one factory in Podolsk (Belarus) manufactured all sewing machines, and one factory in Tallin manufactured all ice skates.[15] Out of 600 manufactured product groups in the USSR, over 430 had a single factory producing the majority of All-Union output.[16] Soviet industry had very few small enterprises. In 1988, almost 95 percent of the industrial labor force worked in enterprises with more than 200 workers, 37.1 percent in enterprises with over 5000 workers.[17] Two representative examples of gigantism would be the Estonian electronics firm *Baltijets* and the Estonian machine building firm *Divitel*. Each of them belonged to the Soviet military-industrial complex, and each had well over 10,000 employees.[18] The industrial giants found it particularly difficult, often impossible, to fit inside a nonmilitary market economy.

The Soviet command economy worked like a military organization, where orders from the general headquarters travel along the chain of command to the soldiers in the field. The process breaks down if the number of individuals to be directed increases beyond a certain point. The chain of command ensures that generals need to direct only colonels, colonels direct only majors, majors direct only captains, and captains direct sergeants. The sergeants deal with the men.

Soviet central planners and the Moscow ministries controlling industries found it much easier to deal with a relatively small number of umbrella organizations instead of a myriad of individual enterprises. "Administrative convenience encouraged and supported the appearance and development of monopolies,"[19] Concerns, trusts, trading organizations, and associations monopolized primarily trade and services. The manufacturing industries, where in many cases one or two enterprises produced the country's total output, were intrinsically monopolistic. Given the Soviet penchant for largeness, the trading and service umbrella organizations reached considerable size. Consequently, the ministries and central planners had to deal with a relatively small number of large monopolies. The emergent market economies had to break them up.

The Soviet society had zero tolerance for unemployment because in a very real sense the heavily subsidized government enterprises provided a way of life for their employees. They lived in company-provided apartments, left their toddlers at the company's day care center, received free medical treatment at the company's clinic, shopped in the company's store, played ball on the company's teams, and spent their vacations at the company's resort. Many enterprises sponsored choruses, dance ensembles, and theatrical groups. Government subsidies covered any shortages of funds necessary to finance all this.

Leif Grahm and Lennart Königson, two Swedish consultants who in early 1991 conducted the first on-site surveys of Baltic industries by foreigners, wrote the following:

Virtually all state enterprises offer extensive range of facilities in which would typically be included free use of clinics, day care center, youth activities, sponsored cultural activities, a range of very well equipped sports clubs. . . . There are almost always stores for staff where hard-to-find items are stocked.[20]

In the Soviet industrial system, a large number of employees in each enterprise worked at providing fringe benefits for the rest. Self-sufficiency was a major goal. In the fall of 1991, I visited the Riga Lighting Engineering Plant, which produced lamps and illuminating fixtures "with shaped bulbs" for the entire USSR. The enterprise employed about 1500 people. I kept wondering how the director, Mr. Vladimir Kraizman, managed to keep track of all the multifarious operations that went far beyond the manufacturing of lighting equipment. A brigade—the Soviets had a predilection for military terminology—built apartment buildings for the enterprise's employees. At the moment, the brigade had nothing to do; nonetheless, the men counted as fully employed. Mr. Kraizman had the funds but lacked the authorization for constructing additional apartment buildings. Other collectives (groups) of employees operated a resort hotel at the seashore, a recreational fishing pond, a hunting lodge some sixty miles from Riga, and a marksmanship range nearby. A special division of very skilled men kept on rebuilding machines, as none had been replaced in the past twenty years. The division head reported with obvious pride that in the case of two large stamping presses imported from Italy in the 1960s, only the original frames had remained intact. Every other part had been rebuilt more than once. Another division ran a day care center and a large kitchen and dining hall for the employees. In addition, the Riga Lighting Engineering Plant fielded soccer and basketball teams. On the other hand, it had no salesmen, no marketing department, and just a minimal office staff. The plant had a labor union, but I could not find out what it did. I saw no safety equipment and nobody wore goggles. According to Mr. Kraizman and his foremen, industrial accidents were extremely rare.

Mr. Kraizman complained about a perennial shortage of labor and the rapidly dwindling supplies of raw materials because the old All-Union distribution system had broken down. It took a great many connections plus ingenuity to keep the plant operating. He leased a part of his labor force from the Red Army. On a shop floor, a large number of young Soviet soldiers in very dirty uniforms worked alongside a large number of young women. They seemed to be having good time but, as the plant manager confirmed, the labor productivity was low. The Lieutenant Colonel nominally in charge of the men did not relish this assignment.

Every Soviet industrial manager had to learn how to cope with bottlenecks and shortages of parts and raw materials. At the same time, there was no need to economize on energy or water usage because public utilities came free of charge or were priced extremely low. As late as December of 1991, Russian oil prices amounted to less than 1 percent of the world's market price. [21] In the old days, many prices used to remain fixed for years. The Soviet experience did not prepare industrial managers for working with prices that reflect actual scarcities.

In addition to a complex and inefficient industrial system, the new republics inherited numerous obsolete plants with run-down equipment plus a small number of factories employing state-of the-art technology. In Riga, the State Microelectronics Experimental Plant, which made computer chips, occupied a brand new, immaculately clean building constructed by a Finnish company. Each floor had a complete air filtration and heat recycling system. White-clad technicians worked with the latest optical equipment at widely dispersed work stations. The managers asserted that the employees were very well paid. The director and the plant manager steered me away, unobtrusively, from the first floor, where allegedly secret work was being done. This plant had all the up-to-date facilities for microelectronic manufacturing.

A more common industrial sight was the State Carton Factory on the outskirts of Riga. It survived only because it employed a large number of severely handicapped workers and paid them extremely low wages. The number of usable machines kept decreasing due to their venerable age and poor maintenance. Inside the dimly illuminated and cluttered plant, grotesque human shapes alongside glue-spattered tables pasted together segments of cardboard cartons distributed by a few limping persons. Everybody had to zigzag among stacks of cardboard sheets. The factory had no local competitors.

After the demise of the Soviet Union, privatization of the economy became the principal challenge. Public debate centered on the forms of ownership. The quality of management received very little attention in part due to the belief that a change of ownership would fix bad management automatically. Many people felt that legions of Western investors could not wait to rush in, offering free management skills and training. The government, these people warned, should be constantly on the watch, making sure that the Westerners did not buy up the country. To the stalwarts of the old regime, the familiar *nomenklatura* managers were perfect by definition; only the economic and political reforms had let them down.

Except for a few outstanding individuals, the mass of the typical Soviet bureaucrats had managed the economy very poorly, finally running it into the ground. In the post-Soviet period, the early successes came to relatively small enterprises started and managed by outsiders, often black marketeers or cooperatives' officials whose entrepreneurial drive could find no outlet under the Soviet planned economy. Most of them were men and women thirty-five years old or younger. The system had not had time to stymie them into docility and passivity. The old folks said that the successful entrepreneurs were stimulated only by greed.

VI

The transformation of a government-managed economy into a market economy requires the demolishing of almost all existing economic institutions. In the USSR, where All-Union and Republican ministries ran industries, no sharp distinction could be made between economic and political institutions. Therefore, the required changes were enormous. Moreover, the ethos, mentality, or mindset of people developed under communism had to be changed if the institutional changes were to succeed.

According to the standards of market economies, the former Soviet Republics started out with considerable psychological, legal, institutional, and technical impediments:

- a penchant for following orders; little individual initiative and an undernourished sense of individual responsibility
- no system for enforcing contracts; inadequate commercial code
- no market for industrial services, including legal services
- popular desire for equality and security irrespective of one's effort; pernicious envy of the more successful
- not so much aversion to as inexperience with risk taking
- a crude command system of management
- unfamiliarity with the concepts and practices of international trade, commercial banking, insurance, and financial investment, made worse by the absence of an indigenous vocabulary of modern commercial terms; no concept of marketing; an accounting system incompatible with the market economy practices in the rest of the world
- little concern with the quality of goods and services
- lack of statistical systems for measuring the rate of inflation and unemployment
- lack of business etiquette, customs, and traditions; no tax-paying ethic
- an attitude, particularly lethal to the electronics industry, that does not embrace or welcome technological change[22]

On the positive side, each of the former Soviet Republics inherited a well-educated labor force and an incredibly patient population, willing to tolerate almost any number of mistakes made by the leaders.

Despite the long list of minuses and the short list of pluses, the former Soviet Republics have experienced some successes. First, all of the new states that emerged from the USSR in 1991 have survived as more or less democratic republics. All of them have held at least one post-Soviet election; the Russian Federation had three. The popular vote unmistakenly shifted to the left. The West may dislike this, but it is difficult to deny that the results represent the popular will. The reformers have not triumphed, but at the same time the socialists and the communists no longer promise a return to the planned command economy. Instead, they want to modify the market economy by keeping several sectors in the hands of the state.

Two prominent Sovietologists and students of the Russian economy, Anders Aslund and Marshall I. Goldman, have written two books with clashing titles. Anders Aslund's 1995 book is called *How Russia Became a Market Economy*. Marshall Goldman calls his 1994 book *Lost Opportunities: Why Economic Reforms in Russia Have Not Worked*. The clashing titles suggest that there exists a considerable disagreement not only about the future course of the Russian Federation's and the other republics' economic and societal progress, but also about what permanent changes have actually taken place. Since 1991, successes have mingled with failures. I will point to some of the successes.

The transformation process from socialism to capitalism has created a sizeable group of very wealthy persons. Members of the top layer vacation on the Mediterranean, shop at Neiman Marcus, and send their children to British public schools. The less wealthy enjoy all the luxuries available at home and make occasional trips to the nearby countries. Perhaps most of the conspicuously wealthy have ties with organized crime, but they do spend large amounts of money supporting various retailing, service, and construction establishments.

Standing on the corner in any of the three Baltic capitals—Riga, Tallin, and Vilnius—or in Moscow or St. Petersburg, one can almost see the economy growing as new stores, offices, restaurants, and bars appear almost daily. In the smaller cities and in the country one sees little evidence of economic growth.

The big cities overflow with retailing establishments, many of them little kiosks that used to carry odd assortments of goods (e.g., auto parts, beer, and pantyhose). There are also modern and well-stocked stores. Some of them go out of business, but most of them survive, even after paying the mafia 10 to 20 percent of the total turnover.[23] Bars seem to be doing particularly well.

Compared to 1991, the number of cars on the streets of Riga in 1994 had approximately doubled. Gone were the old rattletraps that the drivers endeavored to repair on the sidewalks. Even assuming that mafia members owned all the Mercedes and BMW cars, some of the numerous Nissans, Fords, Opels, and Russian-made models on streets must have belonged to nonmafia persons.

The specter of massive unemployment did not materialize. This assertion, however, rests on rather flimsy statistical evidence. Theoretically, the Soviet Union had banished unemployment from the country forever. Consequently, Soviet statistical agencies had no methodology for measuring something that did not exist by definition. They never developed periodic surveys of enterprises or worked out the techniques for catching unemployment with periodic samples of the population. Together with independence came state employment services, where the anticipated unemployed could register for benefits and assistance in job search. The very low benefits served as a poor incentive for registering. Nevertheless, many republics equate the number of unemployed with the number of individuals registered at the state employment service. In the Asian Republics, the Ukraine, Belarus, and the Russian Federation, the official 1993 unemployment rates hovered around 1 percent.[24] Anders Aslund gives the "properly accounted for" unemployment rate for the Russian Federation at the end of 1994 as 7.1 percent. It includes workers on leave without pay.[25] In the Baltic Republics whose statistical agencies have received extensive technical assistance from the International Monetary Fund, the 1993 unemployment rates ranged from 4.2 percent in Lithuania to 8.2 percent in Estonia.[26] The statistical agencies find it difficult to measure underemployment and hidden unemployment (e.g., employees working on half or quarter time, or being put on leave without pay). This keeps people nominally on company payrolls and therefore in company apartments, day care centers, etc.

For the more enterprising residents of the former Soviet Republics, wages have become a diminishing part of income. Working on half or quarter time leaves plenty of hours for moonlighting. Car ownership, fluency in a foreign language, or computer skills offer numerous opportunities for earning additional income. The growth of the skills-intensive services sector, the conspicuous demand for young employees by the joint ventures with foreign companies, and the sharply increasing number of young entrepreneurs have created a major redistribution of income from the old to the young, from the unskilled to the skilled,[27] and from the resigned to the enterprising. The emergent market economy dealt a hard blow to older people. Pensions did not keep up with the cost of living, and the disappearance of the lines in front of stores robbed the retirees from the one advantage they used to enjoy: They did have the time to stand in lines, and to specialize in finding out what was being sold where.[28] The economic value of pensioners to their families diminished with the disappearance of the chronic shortages of consumer goods.

In creating a commercial banking system and other depository institutions, government officials and the nascent bankers found themselves in an unknown territory because nothing like a free-market finance was ever taught in Soviet schools. Accountants and economists had never encountered common stocks, corporate bonds, futures, or mutual funds. Yields or rates of return had never been inputs in anybody's decision making, and interest rates used to remain fixed for decades. Western advisors concentrated their efforts on monetary policy and on the mechanics of banking operations, paying less attention to the safeguards against fraud and the establishing of strict policies for bank audit. Soon all former Soviet Republics faced bank failures and suddenly disappearing depository institutions. Perhaps the most serious debacle occurred in Latvia, where the largest private bank, *Baltija*, collapsed in the spring of 1995. Not long before the collapse, Bank *Baltija* offered 80 percent annual return on selected deposits. Allegedly it had about 200,000 depositors. Similar incidents plagued the entire former USSR. The Russian Federation had the pyramid scheme of the MMM Investment Fund, which promised a guaranteed return of 3000 percent and allegedly had attracted 10 million shareholders.[29]

Bank failures and financial fraud do not epitomize economic success. What these incidents do show is that during a period of severe inflation and economic hardship, a large number of individuals managed to save a part of their incomes. The absence of goods to buy explained the relatively large savings in the USSR, known as monetary overhang. This explanation no longer worked for the post-Soviet republics, where by the early 1993, stores carried a wide selection of domestic and imported goods. Instead, the existence of savings indicates that a large number of individuals had been receiving incomes considerably above the subsistence level. Unfortunately, many of them entrusted their savings to fraudulent, sometimes merely incompetent, depository institutions.

True to the tradition, economic reforms in the former Soviet Union have come from above. Politicians, most of them ex-communists or at least former party members, passed the new laws, conducted fiscal policy, and began privatization while the central banks—independent from the government in some republics, subservient to it in others—effectuated monetary policy. But a government committed to privatization cannot directly create strong and competitive enterprises. Here the initiative must come from the private sector, presently not well endowed with private capital and the entrepreneurial spirit. Some of the new and successful businesspeople have exploited their former *nomenklatura* status and connections. Others have joined up with foreign companies, and a few have struck out on their own. Nonetheless, the total number of new industrial entrepreneurs is too small. What is to be done with the large old plants that no private investor wants? Presently no government knows how to fit them inside a market economy of a democratic country. A widespread belief holds that closing them outright would create unacceptably high unemployment. Given the popular inclination for a large government, it is not difficult to envision a Russian Federation with a large ministry of, say, Defense Industries that would gather under one apron the industrial dinosaurs. Their survival would require huge subsidies that would drag down the entire economy into another period of shortages. Ultimately, all heavily subsidized enterprises must die of natural causes because nobody, including the restructured communist and socialist parties, is willing to repeat the last chapter of the economic scenario that brought down the mighty USSR. Also, too many individuals already own something: apartments, homes, summer cottages, stores, farms, factories, as well as equities and privatization vouchers. Marx would describe this as the bourgeoisification of the proletariat, which makes the return to communism extremely unlikely.

VII

Amid the older buildings of the University of Toronto, in a southward direction from the chapel of Kings College, a victory arch leads into a small square dedicated to the men and women of the University of Toronto who died in World War I. The list of names covers several walls. It is astonishing and a little sad to realize that a single university in sparsely populated Canada had contributed so many young lives to the great overseas war that was to end all wars. The following inscription precedes the engraved roster of names:

TAKE THESE MEN FOR YOUR ENSAMPLES
LIKE THEM REMEMBER THAT PROSPERITY

CAN BE ONLY FOR THE FREE
THAT FREEDOM IS THE SURE POSSESSION OF THOSE ALONE
WHO HAVE THE COURAGE TO DEFEND IT

The second and third lines make an association between prosperity and freedom which would be alien, even repugnant, in the former USSR. The great causes of communism and nationalism transcend prosperity. Being at best a minor accompaniment to freedom, prosperity is not an ideal. It lacks "soul." Fighting and dying in defense of prosperity illustrates capitalism, which reveres individual selfishness and therefore has not won the hearts and minds of many former Soviet citizens devoted to equality. The inalienable right of the pursuit of happiness sounds hollow to people who have been indoctrinated that a full life requires service to a cause that transcends the individual. Instead of receiving money, men and women of outstanding accomplishment in the USSR were awarded medals and honors (e.g., Order of Lenin or Hero of the Soviet Labor). Material reward, "privilege," had to be kept out of sight of the general public. The ninth directorate of the KGB provided perquisites for the politburo and other top-tier leaders. The upper echelon *nomenklatura* lived in special buildings and shopped in special stores, giving the ordinary citizen no opportunity to observe their consumption levels.

The breakup of the USSR created a psychological void, primarily among the Russians. The empire, the quintessential embodiment of Russian pride and accomplishment, was gone. The indigenous peoples of the newly independent states had their nationalism, with its symbols, holidays, official language, and, at least for a few years, the satisfying novelty of a national government. The Russians obviously could not find solace in newly won independence. Currently their own nationalism goes under the name of *Great Russian imperialism*, which is not acceptable to the majority, who fears foreign adventures creating an enormous drain of resources because empires are expensive. It also scares the neighbors of the Russian Federation and makes Europeans and Americans very apprehensive.

I have talked to a number of young Russians who professed to be deeply religious. Did they speak for the majority of their contemporaries? Perhaps. Some of them preferred the Indian religions and shamanism to the traditional Russian Orthodox Church. But the mainline religions are making a comeback. The old cathedrals, reconverted from being grain elevators, concert halls, and museums, are attracting worshipers again, but at a very slow pace. It seems unlikely that in the near future religion will fulfill the ceremonial and emotional functions relinquished by Soviet communism.

Prosperity is undeniably attractive. For most of us it is not difficult to adjust to a greater affluence. And yet, perhaps because they never had it, the ordinary Russians seem to value affluence less highly than the people in the West. Therefore, it is not clear whether the new Russian society will opt for prosperity—potentially the greatest in the world—or another empire.

NOTES

1. Leonid Abalkin, "On New Thinking and Stereotypes of Social Consciousness." *Problems of Economics*, Vol. 34, No. 11 (March 1992), p. 13.

2. The Riga Business School at the Riga Technical University was the first academic institution in the newly independent former Soviet republics that offered a Master of Business Administration (M.B.A.) Program. Funded largely by the U.S. and Canadian government agencies, the Riga Business School grew out of the cooperation between the Riga Technical University, the State University of New York at Buffalo, and, later, the University of Ottawa. The language of instruction is English. The first graduating class received their M.B.A. diplomas in summer of 1995.

3. Elizabeth Tamedly Lenches, "The Legacy of Communism: Poisoned Minds and Souls." *International Journal of Social Economics*, Vol. 20. No. 5-6-7 (1993), p. 19.

4. J. Thad Barnowe, Gundar King, and Eli Berniker, "Personal Values and Economic Transition in the Baltic States." *Journal of Baltic Studies*, Vol. XXIII, No. 2 (Summer 1992), p. 186.

5. Lenches, p. 19.

6. V. Golik, "Privatization, Property Rights, and Motivation." *Problems of Economics*, Vol. 34, No. 11 (March 1992), p. 61.

7. *Diena*, July 4, 1994.

8. *The Baltic Observer*, July 20-26, 1955.

9. *The Baltic Observer*, March 9-15, 1995.

10. Anders Aslund, *How Russia Became a Market Economy.* Washington, D.C.: The Brookings Institution, 1995, p. 168.

11. *Diena*, June 15, 1994.

12. Aleksandr I. Solzhenitsyn, *The Gulag Archipelago, I–III*, New York: Harper & Row, 1974, p. 543.

13. Convicted members of the Russian underworld who collaborated with the labor camp and prison authorities were called "bitches." Those who did not collaborate were known as "honest thieves." *The Gulag Archipelago*, passim.

14. Aslund, p. 168.

15. Leif Grahm and Lennart Königson, *Baltic Industry: A Survey of Potentials and Constraints.* Vastra Frolunda, Sweden: Swedish Development Consulting Partners, 1991, p. 5. The Swedish Ministry of Foreign Affairs, *Economic Survey of the Baltic Republics*, Stockholm, June 1991, p. 294.

16. Maris Martinsons and Krisjanis Valdemars, "Post-Soviet Reforms in Latvia: Early Progress and Future Prospects." *Journal of Economic Studies*, Vol. 19, No. 6 (1992), p. 42.

17. Aslund, p. 152.

18. *Economic Survey of the Baltic Republics*, p. 303.

19. V. V. Ovsienko et al., "Russian Reforms and the Interests of Powerful Social Groups." *Matekon*, Vol. 30, No. 2 (Winter 1993–1994), p. 78.

20. Grahm and Königson, p. 16.

21. Aslund, p. 157.

22. Analyzing the largest Lithuanian computer company, Grahm and Königson concluded that by not mastering the process of change itself, the company became the casualty of change instead of a producer of change. Grahm and Königson, p. 83.

23. Marshall I. Goldman, *Lost Opportunity: Why Economic Reforms in Russia Have Not Worked.* New York: W. W. Norton, 1994, pp. 226–227. Aslund, p. 169.

24. CIA data.

25. Aslund, p. 276.

26. International Monetary Fund data.

27. Aslund, p. 287.

28. Svetozar Pejovich, "The Market for Institutions vs. Capitalism by Fiat." *Kyklos*, Vol. 47, No. 4 (1994), p. 552.

29. *The Economist*, July 30, 1994.

Afterword:
The Russian Presidential Election, June–July 1996

I

The following joke circulated in Riga before the first round of the Russian election. Having cast his vote, President Yeltsin had a few drinks and went to bed. Next morning, an aide woke him up with: "Mr. President, I have good news and bad news." "What's the bad news?" asked the suddenly apprehensive Mr. Yeltsin. "Zyuganov got 55 percent of the popular vote." "Oh God, no! Well, what's the good news?" "You got 65 percent."

In a press conference on May 22, the Communist candidate Gennady Zyuganov warned that if Yeltsin won fraudulently, the Communists might not accept the result. Four days later he stated that the election would not be honest.

As the campaign intensified, Zyuganov repeatedly asserted in his speeches that "communism" actually meant "community." He deplored the soullessness and religious indifference in the West.

The patriarch of the Russian Orthodox Church, Alexey II, urged voters not to support the Communist candidate. "People should not forget the past. What we have seen should never be allowed to reoccur." The Chief Rabbi of Moscow, Adolph Schajevicz, publicly thanked Yeltsin for his assistance in opening a new synagogue in Moscow in July of 1995.

By the eve of the election, Boris Yeltsin had promised at least $2.7 billion for payment of back wages, assistance to local governments, and subsidies to defense industries and social programs.

In an interview broadcasted on CNN, a prominent Russian journalist acknowledged that the media unabashedly rooted for Mr. Yeltsin, not because journalists and editors necessarily agreed with the man and his policies but because a Communist victory would terminate the freedom of the press and their jobs.

A St. Petersburg TV channel conducted an informal survey whether the city's residents preferred the name of St. Petersburg to its former Soviet name of Leningrad. The camera peered into a dance hall filled disproportionately with elderly women. Perhaps in order to save on cosmetics, some of them had applied large quantities of rouge to very small areas on their cheekbones. Most of the women danced with one another. "Which name, ladies, do you prefer?" asked the interviewer. "Leningrad, Leningrad," replied many strident voices.

II

During the last two weeks before June 17, virtually all the world's newsmagazines and TV channels ran cover stories and specials on the Russian election and the main candidates. The tone of the U.S. media seemed to be guardedly pessimistic preparing their readers and viewers for the possibility of a Communist victory. The West European media struck a more optimistic note in the sense that Yeltsin's victory, even though not assured, looked more probable than Zyuganov's. No candidate would garner more than 50 percent of the vote in the first round thus making a runoff election inevitable. Almost everybody agreed that the ultranationalist Zhirinovsky would win third place. The other main candidates, Yavlinsky, Lebed, and Feodorov were lumped together behind Zhirinovsky but ahead of Gorbachev.

The Russian election campaign received relatively limited coverage in the Baltic media. The Latvian press did not conceal the fear of Zyuganov's victory. Just weeks prior the Communist-dominated Russian parliament had voted for a (non-binding) resolution to restore the old USSR. Nevertheless, the editorial writers refrained from openly endorsing any candidate, by and large treating Mr. Yeltsin as the more temperate of the two Russian imperialists in the race.

Reminiscent of the Soviet era when people had good reasons to watch their words, my acquaintances in Riga hesitated to openly discuss the Russian election. When I persisted in asking who would win, my respondents replied that they did not know, could not tell. However, they clearly liked to hear my argument that the young people, the mafiosos, and the successful Russians, who would vote for Yeltsin, should outnumber the pensioners, the old and middle-aged communists, and the embittered and impoverished intellectuals who would vote for Zyuganov.

The candidates themselves and those who spoke for them never tired of repeating that the election, as a contest between the communists and the reformers, would decide Russia's future. The Western media agreed. Despite the seriousness of the contest, the election did not seem to be the dominant preoccupation of most Russians. The electorate was busy. In contrast to the Soviet era, few employees, perhaps none in the private sector, received time off for attending political rallies. On weekends, the election campaigners competed rather unsuccessfully with the pleasurable outdoor activities of the first warm spring days. The winter had been unusually harsh.

To discuss one's politics publicly requires confidence in a democratic system that many Russians, accustomed to constant surveillance by secret police, had not yet developed. The often interviewed "person on the street" frequently refused to reveal his or her surname; many of them gave no response at all. A political rally of like-minded individuals seemed a safer, more congenial setting for showing one's political preferences. The pensioners once had time to stand in long lines in front of state stores. By spring of 1996, the lines were gone leaving the pensioners with ample time to mass in political rallies. Most of them cheered Zyuganov. Yeltsin's people organized their rallies around rock concerts and folk festivals which attracted much younger people. The German newspaper *Deutsche Tagespost* (Würzburg, June 18, 1996), suggested that in his election campaign Mr. Yeltsin had received American advisors and "possibly financial assistance from (American) businesses."

In the Baltic States with their sizeable populations of Russian citizens, neither Yeltsin nor Zyuganov wasted resources in organizing serious political campaigns. "The near abroad"—a term coined by the Russian ministry of foreign affairs—belonged to Zyuganov, the putative restorer of the empire. Out of approximately 60,000 Russian citizens residing in Latvia, 64 percent voted for Zyuganov. He received 62.7 percent of the Russian vote in Estonia and just over 50 percent in Lithuania. The voter participation rate, however, fell under 30 percent versus 70 percent in the Russian Federation. On the sunny but cool election day of June 17, the Russian election precincts in Riga were cheerful places. After casting their ballots, voters lingered over chatting with one another. In one of the courtyards, a number of elderly couples in winter coats danced to music coming from loudspeakers.

III

In retrospect, Yeltsin's victory never was as improbable as many observers asserted. Nevertheless, the Communist party had made a remarkable recovery since its temporary dissolution by Boris Yeltsin in 1991. It has been argued that capitalism is the best system for the reasonably successful but it does not provide very well for the psychological needs of the less successful. Soviet socialism, on the other hand, leveled people. The vaunted egalitarianism included equality of opportunity as well as equality of outcomes except for those to whom *the system* awarded temporary or permanent privilege in the form of spacious apartments, *dachas*, authorization to shop in special stores, foreign travel, etc. Nobody had to work very hard because whatever privilege the system authorized was made easily affordable. For the less privileged members of society the system guaranteed a subsistence level standard of living that included free medical care and education.

The emerging post-Soviet market economy demonstrated all too clearly that the quality of life depended very largely on monetary income. That came as a severe shock to a society that had never measured success in terms of money; only the Americans did so. One's level of income, in turn, depended not on the government's largesse but on luck, connections, skills, enterprise, and hard work. Everybody understood the importance of connections but the rest presented a more or less novel challenge. The rules for advancement, too, had changed. The Soviet system encouraged long-term tenure. Ideally, a young person would start working in a factory after graduation from high school, or after completion of the compulsory military service for males. He or she would retire from the same factory at age 55 if female, or 60 if male. In the course of their 35 or 40 years' tenure, the eminently successful worker would accumulate a number of medals or possibly the honorary title of Hero of Soviet Labor. As the old system broke up and a new system was being born, bigger salaries came to those who had the spunk to change jobs searching for better opportunities.

For the millions of old people whose pensions could not keep up with the rate of inflation, the social safety net dropped below the subsistence level. As the saying goes: "You cannot eat freedom." For pensioners, life had been better under Brezhnev.

Many of the typical stalwarts at communist gatherings wore World War II medals or ribbons on coats shiny with age and multicolored stains. In the West, the veterans of World War II stimulated and largely engineered a period of postwar recovery that led to a new era of unprecedented prosperity. No economic miracle liberated Soviet consumers from ubiquitous and never-ending shortages. By the 1950s, the defeated Germany enjoyed a higher standard of living than the victorious USSR. In the language of the Party, Russian men and women had been building communism and one of the few manifestations of their success was the Soviet empire. Communism had been spreading and the collective effort required for sustaining and defending the empire justified personal deprivations. Renouncing communism near the end of one's essentially selfless life would take away the meaning of that life.

In the old Soviet Union, government subsidies ultimately financed every educational, scientific, and cultural institution. As a consequence, universities, theaters, orchestras, and museums developed huge staffs. Defense-related research sustained numerous large research institutions throughout the country. The Soviet system lavished extensive privileges on academics, scientists, and artists enabling them to lead good, i.e., "privileged" lives.

With the breakup of the Soviet Union, government subsidies either vanished or diminished, and defense industries either shrank or closed down. Cultural institutions had to start paying attention to the size of their audiences. Many distinguished and highly articulate persons lost their jobs. For an unemployed elderly scientist it required no great intellectual effort to perceive the Russian reforms as an "Americanized" hunt for profit that denigrated culture, science, and even civilization. Zyuganov promised a quick return to the good old days with sound values. Even nominally anticommunistic academics in Riga could not help occasionally reveling in their pleasant memories of the fun days as students at the Moscow State University, or the vacation trips with their young families to Crimea or Soviet satellite countries in the 1960s and 1970s, or the interesting conferences in Valdivostok on the Pacific coast of the old USSR.

IV

In the former USSR, attitudes toward reforms and those who stand for or against them break down according to age. The "young people," say, 35 year olds and younger, do not seem to be much different from their American counterparts. Too young to have held important positions under the old regime, they also did not have enough time to develop the habit of excessive goofing off. The foreign firms, joint ventures, and privatized enterprises know this and help-wanted ads often specify that the job applicants must be 35 years old or younger. Most of them have embraced consumerism with the attendant necessity for personal financial success, i.e., they want to make money and many of them succeed. For them, communism and equality are values of the previous, obsolete, generation. This group as a whole is relatively small because the birthrate has been lagging behind the death rate for many years.

The "old people," say, 55 years and older, grew up under communism and imbued its values and mores. For most of them the pull of the past is stronger than the desire to adapt to the new conditions and way of life. However, family histories of members arrested, executed, or deported to the Gulag during Stalin's rule mar even the best memories of the years spent building communism.

The middle group, 35 to 55 years old, whose members occupy the leading positions in every country, consists of men and women with sharply divided loyalties and remarkably changeable philosophies. Opportunists mingle with ardent ideologues. Reformers confront unregenerated communists; very often both have come from the ranks of the former Party *nomenklatura*. In fact, all Russian reforms have been enacted by former members of the *nomenklatura*. Most business leaders as well as the shadowy mafia leaders started out in the *nomenklatura*. The political preferences of the middle group defied pre-election predictions. In the first round, their vote turned out to be almost evenly split between Yeltsin and Zyuganov.

After the General Election Committee had finished counting the votes of the first round, Boris Yeltsin had won 35.1 percent, Gennady Zyuganov 32.0 percent, and Alexander Lebed 14.7 percent. The other candidates lagged far behind but the liberal reformer Grigory Yavlinsky had attracted more votes—7.4 percent—than the ultra-nationalist firebrand Vladimir Zhirinovsky with 5.8 percent.

V

The only real surprise in the first round of the Russian election was the 14.7 percent of the vote received by General Lebed. After he joined President Yeltsin's camp, a Communist loss in the second round became almost certain.

As a soldier and politician, General Lebed has one peculiar quality shared to some extent also by Mr. Yeltsin: people like to make up legends about him. They see in him something more than dispassionate observers are able to detect because something in his personality, demeanor, and appearance works on the public's imagination.

General Lebed has been called unsophisticated, uncosmopolitan, uncouth, even ignorant but never inarticulate. He says memorable things often laced with heavy sarcasm, a peculiarly Russian variety of humor. Yes, he would lead a regiment into the rebellious Chechnya "provided that regiment was made up of children and uncles of officials and children and uncles of members of the government."[1] Or: "Russian culture must prevail over American chewing gum."[2] Or the pungently nationalistic and arrogant: "I shall never serve tsars, commissars, or presidents. They are mortal men who come and go. I serve only the Russian state and the Russian people who are eternal."[3] Or the cynical: "Most Russians do not care whether they are ruled by communists, fascists or men from Mars as long as they can buy six kinds of sausage and plenty of inexpensive vodka."[4] He used a memorable campaign slogan: "I have already ended one war." This refers to the armed conflict in Moldova where in 1991 and 1992 the Moldovans fought the secessionist Russians and Ukrainians in the Transdniester region. As commander of the Russian Federation's Fourteenth Army stationed in Moldova, General Lebed achieved an armistice by having his troops shoot first and ask questions later. Apparently the Fourteenth Army shot more Moldavians than Russians, but the armistice still stands.

General Alexander Lebed was born of Don cossack stock in 1950 in Novocherkask, Southern Russia. The *cossacks*, Russians or Ukrainians by origin and language, settled along the south and southeastern frontier of Russia as early as the sixteenth century. When serfdom ruled in Russia, the cossacks remained free but they had to give military service to the Russian state. Military service was obligatory to all men for 20 years beginning at the age of 18. For centuries cossacks fought as the vanguard in Russia's wars and served as the internal security force vigorously suppressing internal rebellions and strikes. Great Russian writers, including Tolstoy and Pushkin, celebrated the cossack feats of arms and their free way of life. Communism did not appeal to the cossack independent spirit. Their regiments formed the core of the anticommunist White Armies in the Russian Civil War. Passive resistance continued throughout the 1920s. The literary classic of the Soviet Union, Mikhail Sholokhov's *And Quiet Flows the Don* deals with the difficult collectivization of the cossack lands. But even for communist historians, the cossacks embodied the best in Russian early military history. The military profession thrives on tales of legendary feats of soldiering, and being a descendent of the fearless, if cruel, horsemen of the steppe enhances the image of any Russian officer.

At the age of 19, Lebed enlisted in the paratroopers. He fought in Afghanistan as a battalion commander winning the order of the Red Star. Next he commanded an elite airborne division that in 1989 and 1990 participated in the bloody suppression of nationalist demonstrations in Georgia and Azerbaijan. During the August 1991 putsch, Lebed's paratroopers quickly sided with President Yeltsin. His reward was the command of the Fourteenth Army in Moldova.

General Lebed's vehement opposition to the war in Chechnya led to a bitter conflict with the Defense Minister General Pavel Grachev, his former boss in Afghanistan, and also with President Yeltsin. At least with his words, General Lebed showed totally unprecedented insubordination by calling the Defense Minister a diplomatic general and a prostitute, and urging President Yeltsin to retire and grow strawberries. The President extolled General Lebed's peace keeping accomplishments, but fired him in June of 1995.

The retired Lieutenant General Lebed won an easy election to the Russian Duma as a member of the Congress of Russian Communities. He left his party after it refused to finance his presidential bid.

By the time General Lebed mounted his presidential campaign in early 1996, he was quickly becoming a legend. General Lebed was the only teetotaler among his peers. In the English equivalents of corresponding Russian phrases, the people's general called spade a spade, told it like it was, minced no words, and kowtowed to nobody. He promised order.

There is a country called Russia where people suffer from lies, corruption, and banditry. I want to wipe this dirt off the face of Russia.[5]

Today we have freedom, but no order. Others offer order without freedom. I want that our state had both, freedom and order.[6]

He also promised to take the Russian Army out of Chechnya and let a referendum determine its future. Russia should have a much smaller, professional army which would mean getting rid of the old diplomatic generals. As for Communism:

We have an old ideology that has spent itself. We have paid for it with colossal amounts of blood and suffering. There are new ideas. It is true that they have been realized in a noxious form, but they are new and therefore the future belongs to them.[7]

The day after the first round of the election, President Yeltsin appointed General Lebed to the position of Secretary of the National Security Council and national security advisor to the president. The National Security Council meets behind closed doors and formulates military and internal security policies for the Russian Federation. The twelve permanent members include the president, the prime minister, the defense minister, senior military commanders, and chairmen of selected Duma committees. The full membership of the National Security Council has never been disclosed.

In a press conference after his appointment, General Lebed demonstrated a broad view of what constituted national security. He suggested that in the present critical situation, food imports, the worsening interregional relations in Russia, the flight of capital abroad, and even the return on investment had national security ramifications. His principal rival, Prime Minister Viktor Chernomyrdin, did not see things the same way.

Next Mr. Yeltsin, searching for votes, executed the most dramatic coup of this election. He ousted four of his long-time loyalists, commonly described as economic conservatives and the War Party. Gone was General Alexander Korzhakov, the commander of the president's personal security detachment and said to be Yeltsin's closest personal friend. Also gone were Mikhail Berzukov, the head of the Federal Security Service, formerly KGB; Oleg Seskovets, First Deputy Prime Minister in charge of the military-industrial complex; and General Pavel Grachev, the Defense Minister. The departures of the defense and the intelligence chief boosted General Lebed's authority but the removal of four economic and political conservatives also gratified the liberal *JaBloko Party* of Grigory Yavlinsky, who would ultimately ask his followers to support Yeltsin. After this coup, President Yeltsin did not need to campaign—and he didn't—causing persistent rumors that his health had collapsed.

General Lebed thought that 70 percent of his followers would vote for Mr. Yeltsin. He was probably right. In the second and final round of the presidential election, Yeltsin received 54 percent of the votes, Zyuganov 40 percent. Six percent checked off "None of the above." Most Russian citizens in Riga still voted for Zyuganov but the voter participation rate was lower than before.

VI

What did the election mean? In which direction will the Russian Federation go? The election result clarified the future only insofar as it removed some elements of the past. It seems certain that the Soviet-type communism is dead and shall not be resurrected. Death due to old age will increasingly decimate the minority that still clings to it. Zyuganov, like the communist leaders before him, could not come to terms with the information age symbolized by the ubiquitous computer. It will not do in 1996 to argue, as Zyuganov did, that Stalin had no more than half-a-million victims and most of them were party members. These are lies that belong in the same category as denial of the holocaust. They persuade only those who select information exclusively on the basis of ideological content.

The free market has opened up opportunities for ordinary people which did not exist under socialism. The idea of personal success and wealth without the permission of the government or the Party has intoxicated many Russians. A large number of women have demonstrated an unexpected aptitude for business. For some of them, success in business also means independence of alcoholic and abusive males. They would be loath to give this up for the return of communism. As for the less successful members of society, they do not have a commanding voice.

The Russian reforms will continue, led by former members of the Party's *nomenklatura* who, in Zyuganov's words, have remade themselves into "democrats." General Lebed, too, used to talk about men who went to bed with totalitarianism and woke up next to democracy. Because the communist threat has dissipated, the West will be more supportive of the Russian economy.

To a considerable extent, the election served as a referendum of the war in Chechnya. No major candidate defended it. How soon the war ends will depend on the authority given to General Lebed, who shows a clear disposition for quick and decisive solutions. Next to law and order, his platform called for ending the war.

A Russian proverb says that two bears cannot live in the same cave. General Lebed may or may not be President Yeltsin's crown prince but he has rivals, first among them the Prime Minister Viktor Chernomyrdin. Whether the President will tolerate an outright power struggle in the Kremlin probably depends on his state of health. During the election campaign the visible evidence of President Yeltsin's physical condition varied sharply. Until the first round of the election, the public heard Mr. Yeltsin's vigorous voice on the radio and TV and saw him dancing with his constituents as he visited many regions and cities of the Russian Federation. Between the first and second round he virtually disappeared making just one live TV appearance in front of a ballot box. Zyuganov's camp accused the President of hiding a serious and incapacitating illness, his own people countered by saying that the President was merely saving an over-taxed voice.

Mr. Yeltsin's brief appearance in front of the ballot box showed how personal impressions of the same event can differ. Most Western journalists reported that he looked sick and tired. Their Latvian colleagues felt that Mr. Yeltsin looked fit and talked in an animated fashion. To me he appeared wooden, as a person who wears a body cast. But I saw him only on TV for less that two minutes, and most 65-year old men do not have very flexible bodies. The President's "official" medical history, never released in Russia, already lists two heart attacks. Clearly his physical condition will remain a major issue during his second term.

The Russian presidential election took place in the world's largest country, sprawling over eleven time zones. Nothing in Russia's history had prepared it for a democratic multi-party election. And yet, no complaints were made by the many outside observers or the losing parties about serious irregularities. Everybody accepted the decision of the voters. All ballots were counted by hand; nonetheless the results arrived expeditiously at the General Election Committee's offices in Moscow. The election was conducted in a highly profes-sional manner where even the mistrusted exit polls turned out to be remarkably accurate. The voter participation rate did not reach the institutionalized almost-hundred-percent-level of the former USSR but the 65 to 70 percent of the eligible votes cast surpassed the voting rates in the United States.

The election offered an example that Russians can carry out anything they set out to do. Historically, the Russian people have often set out to do things, willingly or under the government's compulsion, that did not make them and their neighbors better off. The individual always had to be subordinated either to the abstract cause of communism as defined by the Communist party, or to the quasi-religious concept of Holy Russia personified by the tsar. Perhaps the summer election of 1996 has marked a turning point in Russian history from a cause-serving collectivism to more individual-centered values.

NOTES

1. Quoted in *Der Spiegel*, June 24, 1996.

2. Quoted in *The Economist*, June 22–28, 1996.

3. Quoted in *Der Spiegel*, June 24, 1996.

4. Ibid.

5. Quoted in *Diena*, June 20, 1996.

6. Ibid.

7. Ibid.

Bibliography

Abalkin, Leonid. "On New Thinking and Stereotypes of Social Consciousness." *Problems of Economics*. Vol. 34, No. 11 (March 1992), 6–19.

Āboltiņš, Jānis. *Biju biedrs, tagad kungs*. Rīga: Jakubāna un Hānberga bibliotēka, 1992.

Aganbegyan, Abel. *Inside Perestroika: The Future of the Soviet Economy*. New York: Harper & Row, 1989.

Allworth, Edward. *The Modern Uzbeks*. Stanford: Hoover Institution Press, 1990.

Arbatov, Georgi. *The System: An Insider's Life in Soviet Politics*. New York: Times Books, 1992.

Aslund, Anders. *How Russia Became a Market Economy*. Washington, D.C.: The Brookings Institution, 1995.

Barnowe, Thad J. et al. "Personal Values and Economic Transition in the Baltic States." *Journal of Baltic Studies*. Vol. 23, No. 2 (1992), 179–190.

Beliaeva, Liudmila. "Russia Confronts a Historic Choice." *Problems of Economic Transition*. Vol. 37, No. 4 (August 1994), 14–29.

Bergson, Abram. "The USSR Before the Fall: How Poor and Why." *The Journal of Economic Perspectives*. Vol. 5, No. 4 (Fall 1991), 29–44.

Bērzkalns, Valentīns. *Latviešu dziesmu svātku vēsture*. New York: Grāmatu draugs, 1965.

Campbell, Robert W. "Economic Reforms in the USSR and Its Successor States." *Making Markets*. Eds. Shafiqul Islam and Michael Mandelbaum. New York: Council of Foreign Relations Press, 1993.

Dreifelds, Juris. "Intervija an Anatolu Gorbunovu." *Baltiešu forums*. Vol. 4, No. 2 (1987), 40–50.

Ericson, Richard E. "The Classical Soviet-Type Economy: Nature of the System and Implications for Reform." *The Journal of Economic Perspectives*. Vol. 5, No. 4 (Fall 1991), 11–27.

Felshman, Neil. *Gorbachev, Yeltsin and the Last Days of the Soviet Empire.* New York: St. Martin's Press, 1992.

Frydman, Roman et al. *The Privatization Process in Russia, Ukraine and the Baltic States.* CEU Privatization Reports, Vol. 2. Budapest, London, New York: Central European University Press, 1993.

Gale, Robert and Thomas Hauser. *Final Warning: The Legacy of Chernobyl.* New York: Warner Books, 1988.

Ģērmanis, Uldis. *Zināšanai: raksti par mūsu un padomju lietām.* Stockholm: Ziemeļzvaigzne, 1985.

Goldman, Marshall. *Lost Opportunity: Why Economic Reforms in Russia Have Not Worked.* New York and London: W. W. Norton, 1994.

Golik, V. "Privatization, Property Rights, and Motivation." *Problems of Economics.* Vol. 34., No. 11 (March 1992), 55–65.

Gorbachev, Mikhail. *Perestroika: New Thinking for Our Country and the World.* New York: Harper & Row, 1987.

Grahm, Leif and Lennart Königson. *Baltic Industry: A Survey of Potentials and Constraints.* Vastra Frolunda, Sweden: Swedish Development Consulting Partners, 1991.

Gwertzman, Bernard and Michael T. Kaufman (eds.). *The Collapse of Communism.* New York: Times Books, 1990.

Harmstone, Teresa Rakowska. *Russia and Nationalism in Central Asia, the Case of Tadzhikistan.* Baltimore and London: The Johns Hopkins Press, 1970.

Kaiser, Robert G. *Why Gorbachev Happened.* New York: Simon & Schuster, 1992.

Kalniņš, Viktors. "Daudznacionālā, bet ne vienotā . . . " *Latvija šodien 1983.* Rockville, Md.: World Federation of Free Latvians. No. 11 (November 1983), 108–117.

Kornai, Janos. *The Road to a Free Economy: Shifting From a Socialist System: The Example of Hungary.* New York and London: W. W. Norton, 1990.

Latvijas valsts Statistikas komiteja. *Statistikas gadagrāmata '89.* Riga: 1990.

Lenches, Elizabeth Tamedly. "The Legacy of Communism: Poisoned Minds and Souls." *International Journal of Social Economics.* Vol. 20, No. 5–6–7 (1993), 14–34.

Lieven, Anatol. *The Baltic Revolution: Estonia, Latvia, Lithuania and the Path to Independence.* New Haven and London: Yale University Press, 1993.

Mandelbaum, Michael. "Coup De Grace: The End of the Soviet Union." *Foreign Affairs.* Vol. 71, No. 1 (1992), 164–183.

Martinsons, Maris and Krisjanis Valdemars. "Post-Soviet Reform in Latvia: Early Progress and Future Prospects." *Journal of Economic Studies.* Vol. 19, No. 6 (1992), 33–52.

Medvedev, Grigori. *The Truth About Chernobyl.* New York: Basic Books, 1991.

Moskoff, William. *Hard Times: Impoverishment and Protest in Perestroika Years.* Armonk, N.Y.: M. E. Sharpe, 1993.

Mould, Richard. *Chernobyl: The Real Story.* Oxford: Pergamon Press, 1988.

O'Brien, John C. "The Evils of Soviet Communism and Other Critical Essays: Part 1, Introduction." *International Journal of Social Economics.* Vol. 21, No. 2-3-4 (1994), 4-13.

Olcott, Martha Brill. "The Lithuanian Crisis." *Foreign Affairs.* Vol. 69, No. 3 (1990), 30-45.

Ovsienko, V. V. et al. "Russian Reforms and the Interests of Powerful Social Groups." *Matekon.* Vol. 30, No. 2 (Winter 1993-1994), 77-93.

Pejovich, Svetozar. "The Market for Institutions vs. Capitalism by Fiat: The Case of Eastern Europe." *Kyklos.* Vol. 47, No. 4 (1994), 519-529.

Rakitskaia, Galina. "Defending the Interests of Working People Under Property Reform." *Problems of Economic Transition.* Vol. 37, No. 7 (November 1994), 28-43.

Rauda, Māris. " 'Tev, Stāļin, sekojam par lielo cīņu takām'." *Latvija šodien 1985.* Rockville, Md.: World Federation of Free Latvians. No. 13 (December 1985), 39-44.

Read, Piers P. *Ablaze: The Story of the Heroes and Victims of Chernobyl.* New York: Random House, 1993.

Rywkin, Michael, *Moscow's Muslim Challenge.* Revised ed. Armonk, N.Y.: M. E. Sharpe, 1990.

Senn, Alfred Erich. "The Crisis in Lithuania, January 1991: A Visitor's Account." *Newsletter, Association for the Advancement of Baltic Studies.* Vol. 15, No. 1 (March 1991).

Shen, Raphael. *Restructuring the Baltic Economies: Disengaging Fifty Years of Integration with the USSR.* Westport, CT and London: Praeger, 1994.

Solovyov, Vladimir and Elena Klepikova. *Behind the High Kremlin Walls.* New York: Dodd, Mead & Co., 1986.

——— . *Boris Yeltsin: A Political Biography.* New York: G. P. Putnam's Sons, 1992.

Solzhenitsyn, Aleksandr I. *The Gulag Archipelago, I-III.* New York: Harper & Row, 1974.

Spekke, Arnolds. *History of Latvia.* Stockholm: M. Goppers, 1957.

Strunskis, Viktors. " 'Padomju cilvēka' ieaugšana sabiedrībā." *Latvija šodien 1983.* Rockville, Md.: World Federation of Free Latvians. No. 11 (November 1983), 121-127.

The Swedish Ministry of Foreign Affairs. *Economic Survey of the Baltic Republics.* Stockholm: June 1991 (Mimeo).

Willis, David K. *Klass: How Russians Really Live.* New York: St. Martin's Press, 1975.

Index

About the Author

GEORGE J. NEIMANIS is professor and former chair of the Department of Economics and Commerce at Niagara University. He served as an advisor to the Latvian Parliament and as a visiting faculty member at the Riga Business School.

CPSIA information can be obtained
at www.ICGtesting.com
Printed in the USA
BVHW07*2025101018
529738BV00008B/405/P